I AM MUSIC
My Journey With Dimash Kudaibergen
THE BEST SINGER IN THE WORLD

Pamela McGee Wilkinson

I AM MUSIC
Copyright © 2021 by Pamela McGee Wilkinson

Library of Congress Control Number: 2021902598
ISBN-13: Paperback: 978-1-64749-416-2
Hardback: 978-1-64749-417-9
ePub: 978-1-64749-367-7

All rights reserved. No part of this publication may be reproduced, distributed, or transmitted in any form or by any means, including photocopying, recording, or other electronic or mechanical methods, without the prior written permission of the publisher or author, except in the case of brief quotations embodied in critical reviews and certain other noncommercial uses permitted by copyright law.

Although every precaution has been taken to verify the accuracy of the information contained herein, the author and publisher assume no responsibility for any errors.

Printed in the United States of America

GoToPublish LLC
1-888-337-1724
www.gotopublish.com
info@gotopublish.com

Contents

ABOUT THE AUTHOR v
PREFACE 1
I AM MUSIC 4
ABOUT I AM MUSIC 7
I AM MUSIC - THE POEM 20
    I AM MUSIC 20
    DIMASH QUDAIBERGEN 23
    THE RECEIVING PLACE 24
    A MAGNIFICENT OBSESSION - preface 26
    A MAGNIFICENT OBSESSION 27
    THERE'S SOMETHING WRONG WITH HIM! .. 29
    DIGITAL DIMASH MAGIC 31
    THE LETHAL WEAPON 32
    THE MASTER'S REPAIR 34
    THE DIMASH SMILE 35
    A CHRISTMAS SCARF 38
    THE PHOTO REVISITED 40
    BREAKING THE NEWS TO MOM 41
    ASTROLATRY 42
    PAM WONDERS.......IS DIMASH OUR MUSE? . 43
    THE CHOIR IS HERE! 45
    THE SCULPTOR 47

THE SCULPTOR'S MASTERPIECE	51
UNFORGETTABLE DAYS	59
BEFORE AND AFTER	61
SUPERCALIFRAGILISTICWITH DIMASHITOSIS	62
TO BE(ARD) OR NOT TO BE(ARD) THAT IS THE QUESTION	64
THINGS I DON'T UNDERSTAND	66
CURIOUS BY NATURE	67
A DAY IN THE LIFE OF A DEAR	68
DIMASHITOSIS DIAGNOSIS	71
DIMASHITIS	73
THE ARNAU BREAKDOWN	77
JUST A GUY FROM KAZAKHSTAN/ THE PEAR POEM	78
PERSON(ALIZED) LICENSE PLATE	80
I AM MUSIC MY LICENSE PLATE	80
MY LEAF POEM	81
A LEAGUE OF HIS OWN	82
THE FATHER OF SONGS	83
THE GOLDEN THROAT	84
VERY PERSONAL JOURNAL ENTRY	85
WORD SEARCH	87
DIMASH FLYER	88
PAM'S FAVORITES IN ALPHABETICAL ORDER IN ORDER TO AVOID FAVORITISM OF ANY KIND	89
DEARS' COMMENTS	90

ABOUT THE AUTHOR

Pamela's introduction into writing began in high school when the English class was challenged to write a biography about a member of their class. Class members were asked to call them up and interview them over the phone and collect interesting details about their childhood, hobbies, etc.

A week after the biographies were turned in, the teacher announced that she was impressed with many of the biographies but one stood out as the best example of capturing the personality of her subject and also utilizing her apparent natural skills as an interviewer. Her teacher informed her she should consider using her writing skills in the future.

As the years followed, Pamela would find many opportunities to use her writing skills namely; poetry, skits, newsletters, roadshows and writing new lyrics for existing music for plays and talent shows. She also interviewed interesting people in her Memphis, Tennessee community that were published in local newspapers.

She currently lives in the St. George, Utah area. She is the widow of Kenneth M. Wilkinson, mother of three and grandmother of seven.

She is also the author of the book *"The Princess of Cyres Hill"*

"The author will be donating in memory of her late husband, a percentage of the royalties from the sale of this book to the Alzheimer's Association, Utah Chapter, Draper, Utah."

This book is dedicated to Emma Powell McGee

A nurse and the poet laureate of the hospital in Columbia, Louisiana circa 1940's to 1960s. Emma was my grandmother, my father's mother, and besides her amazing southern chicken and dumplings she shared during our visits to her home, she shared her poetry. She never had to get out a copy of the poems, as she knew them all by heart. I would sit on her bed along with my siblings, Mike, Bobbie, Pat and Mark as she quoted poem after poem. I loved her style and thought that it was amazing that she could make words rhyme so perfectly and inject the right amount of humor. Years later I copied her style and therefore dedicate this book to her legacy.

Thanks Gee Gee for the poetry and the dumplings.

Pamela McGee Wilkinson

Acrylic cover of Dimash by Megan Warner warnemeg67.wixsite.com

PREFACE

People who excel at something to the point of disbelief from the rest of the world are so rare it's like finding the proverbial needle in a haystack. But geniuses or academic wonders, superb athletes, actors or actresses who receive award after award from their peers, are discovered then lauded but soon someone smarter or more talented comes along. Someone is always out there being born, being raised to excel either by parents or by his or her own motivation. No matter how they reach that pinnacle and how long and how hard they worked to achieve that height, someone, someday, will move them aside and say "Yes, but look at me. It's my turn now". That's great for them but the former "best of whatever" hopefully will still hold some respect and admiration for their legacy. Many of them do.

In the "singing world" there have been many who have achieved fame and recognition and wealth and they have even exceeded what they dreamed of becoming. They had knowledgeable promoters, agents, managers, producers, and numerous others who helped them along the way, including enthusiastic fans, to ultimate success.

I've seen lists of the best singers in the world and all I can say is that they pale in comparison to the singer of whom I am a fan. As a matter of fact, now that I know what this singer is capable of with his range, which is unlimited and his performance quality and his expertise in all things musical, those "best singers in the world" lists look fairly sad. Sorry, but it's a fact for me **and** many of the people around the world reading this journal of mine will enthusiastically share my sentiments.

We have discontinued following those other singers because now we want to be entertained by the best entertainer in the world. Why wouldn't we? We can still "visit" our former favorites but we don't want to "live" there anymore. We have set up house with this young man and we are not going anywhere. He is in our head and in our hearts and he is there to stay.

Dimash Kudaibergen, his professional name, is not a household name in my country. Yet! But when whatever happens that has America discussing him at every water cooler or in every break room at work, or on all the social medias or network channels etc. finally happens, millions will be astounded and ask themselves…. "Why don't I know about this guy? Where have I been? Where has he been?"

Welcome to a fan's perspective of her two-year journey with the Best Singer in the World. I represent millions.

Pamela McGee Wilkinson

OBVIOUS LACK OF PHOTOS

Due to copyright issues concerning use of photos on the internet for book publishing and the issue that permission has to be granted by the owner of the photos…..

I would have loved to have included several photos that inspired many of my poems but alas, my attempts to reach Dimash through his IG and his emails and attempts to alert others to my photo needs for this book did not result in any responses. Therefore, the picture I took of my Christmas scarf is the only one I was allowed to use that inspired a poem. I understand that he and his manager and friends are inundated with requests of all kinds and can't possibly respond to all of them and due to the volume of communications they all receive, some of these requests will go undiscovered. I am still feeling blessed and privileged to publish my poems and other writings. So this will not be a "picture book". Most of the dears know where to find the photos that inspired these poems because they have become some of our favorites.

So if you can imagine Playboy magazine without the pictures, then this is it. Sorry for the questionable reference but I had to go for the joke, again.

Pamela McGee Wilkinson
January 2021

I AM MUSIC

My Journey with Dimash Kudaibergen.... The Best Singer in the World!

PAM'S PERSONAL JOURNEY JOURNAL

I am a fan, a Dear of **Dimash Kudaibergen**, a singer with a capital **S.I.N.G.E.R.!** To begin, let me assure you, I am not crazy. I am *obsessed*. People who are obsessed can and do go about their normal lives and routines. Eat, sleep, live, love, hate, cry, laugh and hopefully a lot, sing, dance, clog, jog, walk, run, work, move, breathe etc. They do not need psychiatric help or any intervention of any kind. They just spend an inordinate amount of time obsessing about a thing or a person(s). Leave them alone. They'll be okay. I promise. The object of my obsession blasted himself up and out, like the proverbial rocket ship heading out to space, in very early 2017 on a Chinese competition show called The Singer.

This is my fanbook and it is comprised of posts to my Facebook fan pages in 2020 and a few in 2021. Only I didn't realize that I was compiling a fanbook at the time or that I had so many entries in the form of poetry, skits, scenarios of several kinds or just some musings where I go on and on about this guy. I have had requests from fellow dears to write a book and include my writings. In this journal/fanbook

I try to explain the unexplainable. Have you ever tried to do that? It's like Halloween….scary and fun at the same time.

If someone would have told me three years ago that I would be obsessed with a singer from Kazakhstan and would publish my musings about him, I would have asked them which mental institution they preferred…the local one or the really fancy one up north. A more likely scenario would be the following: My guardian angel, my GA, comes to me in some mysterious way, say, three years ago, and says…..

GA: Pamela Kay McGee Wilkinson?

Me: (Not shocked by his presence) Yes. That's me.

GA: Great. I've got the right one. I have something to tell you about your future.

Me: Okay, go ahead. I'm listening.

GA: I'm glad you're listening but you should be sitting down too.

Me: Fine! Fine! I'm sitting. So whatcha got?

GA: In the very near future, we are talking roughly 2019 through 2020…..

Me: Wait! Roughly 2019 to 2020? I thought you GAs had everything pinned down to the second.

GA: Actually no. That's a myth. Things happen beyond our control all the time and we are only allowed to come down and deliver news that is a sure thing.

Me: So apparently you are here to tell me that my news is a sure thing?

GA: Yes. Sounds like we're on the same page.

Me: Okay then, let's have it.

GA: During those aforementioned years, you will start to follow a singer from Kazakhstan.

Me: Follow him? Like stalking him? Going wherever he goes? Does he live in Utah? Is he my neighbor? Is he cute? What kind of music does he sing? Is he as good as, say, Michael Buble or Justin Bieber? Wait! Kazakhstan? Is that a suburb of St. George I don't know about?

GA: No. No. Give me a minute to explain. You will discover him while watching a CBS variety competition show and this singer will send you on a two-year journey of discovery that will consume your leisure time to the point of obsession. Then you'll write a book about it and release it in 2021. Later.

Me: What!?!? That doesn't sound like me.

GA: You'll see. Have a nice day. (GA leaves the same way he arrived)

Me: Wow! That was interesting. But I still don't know if he's cute or not. Or his name!! Hmmmm!

First of all, since this is my journal, let me introduce myself. I am **but one** member of a society of fanatics riding on the Dimash train or spaceship. We have our tickets and they are stamped and our bags are packed for every situation and we have the international power adapters to prove it. We are all on this journey with him and we talk about it a lot. I am just a regular middle-aged gal (if I live to be about 135 years old) who is living in the southwestern part of the State of Utah, USA which is practically a doppelganger to the singer's beautiful homeland of Kazakhstan. (Just an aside.) And I am just one of the millions who can't for the life of us understand what this man has done to our lives. I have been on this journey with Dimash for two years and I've done it all right here in my home. I did leave once on this journey and that was to go to New York but no international power adapter needed. More about New York later.

ABOUT I AM MUSIC

When you make a statement like that you better have facts or something akin to facts to back it up. I DO! If hundreds of first time listeners to Dimash who are vocal coaches are any indication of how great the man is, then here you go.

"He's not human."

"What planet is he from?"

"I've never experienced anything like him."

"Find me a better singer and I'll eat my socks."

"I had no idea that a human voice could do that."

"There is no disconnect between his soul and his music."

"HE IS, DARE I SAY IT, THE BEST SINGER IN THE WORLD."

Typical first time reactions from them and I have watched hundreds of regular people like me with very little vocal knowledge react to him. And even if you use the word "otherworldly" because we all do, it's beginning to sound limited instead of limitless. I have no idea how many fans he has and I don't know if it's possible to even know an exact number because it's growing every second. But I'm guessing it's millions and millions of course.

DIMASH IS MUSIC. HE LIVES MUSIC. BREATHES IT IN AND EXHALES IT OUT IN THE FORM OF SINGING AND EMOTING AND LEAVING **YOU** BREATHLESS! HE DOES IT ON PURPOSE! DANG THAT MAN! AND FOR ALL INTENTS AND PURPOSES….*HE IS OBSESSED* TOO.

The reaction exclamations range from "Oh My Gosh!" (G-rating) to words I don't want to type much less repeat (R-rating). SHOCK is the first go-to-emotional response. Then without any heads up for these mostly physical responses …BAM!…here come the goose bumps, chills, jaw drops, a certain amount of frustration (but the good kind) and then even grown men are crying like babies. Sorry guys but you are. The most popular word to escape from their mouths after their first, second, third, etc. reaction is 'SPEECHLESS'. The only critique that could be considered *critical* is…"That was too short. I wanted more. I wasn't ready for it to be over." Me either, Vocal Coach, me either!

This is not a biography of the Kazakh singer, composer, MV director, multi-instrumentalist, dancer, and lately a digital concert producer, countryman/patriot and humanitarian. There are other talents and traits but I'll keep you in suspense or leave it to the biographer. That is not my place. In time his biography will be written but it will be by someone he chooses. At age twenty-six (at the time of this particular journal) he still has way too many songs to sing and stories to tell. He has more compositions to write and many of them floating around in his head as I type this. More collaborations with the best in the business. He has untold hours of vocal training and practice to keep his instrument in marvelous otherworldly shape so he can surprise us with more techniques no one has ever heard of before *much less tried*. Vocal coaches say that at 26 he has not reached his prime and that, ladies and gentlemen, is *scary*. Thank you for that hard work DK! It shows and we appreciate it. We are always showing him our appreciation. (Cuz us Dears are great!)

ABOUT HIS VOCAL RANGE

I once considered myself an okay singer. I "practiced singing" when my Dad used to pay me a quarter every time I sang, "You are my Sunshine" to him. I didn't like the song necessarily but I loved the quarter. Then the Beatles arrived in my early teens and I sang and memorized every one of their songs. But I'd have to say once I sang them 100 times or so I was ready to move on. Still loved the Beatles but tired of singing their songs. For me they became good memories but been-there-and-done-that memories, I guess. Once, my oldest daughter in her teen years asked me..."Mom, what was it like to live during the *Beatles' days*?" That was hard to answer but I did. Explaining *Dimash days* is very hard to do and it can take up so much of your time and the listener's time.

If I guessed how many times I've heard S.O.S. or Sinful Passion or dozens of others, I could be off by a few hundred. I KNOW I've heard S.O.S. and Sinful Passion more than a thousand times apiece. (If you are reading this and you are not a true Dear, you are probably asking yourself..."How can you NOT be tired of those songs by now?" We don't know. Ask someone smarter than us.) His vocal range is not two octaves or three. It's not even five. The man kindly refuses to reveal the actual number to us. Why? Is he hiding something from us*? Is it true he came from another planet that is so advanced that they laugh at octaves and registers? Child's play.* But vocal coaches have said as much as a D8 to D10 on the high notes is possible and on the low end...he has made vocal fry another octave but I do understand it's a register. I've looked up lots of info about octaves and registers and all those other ways to describe them and I feel like I'm trying to learn the Kazakh language. So enough about my stupidity or lack of knowledge on this subject. All you have to do is witness some of those hundreds of vocal coaches who break it down for you and then you feel pretty impressed about the man's vocal gymnastics. No, actually, you feel overwhelmed. Gob smacked! Thank you British Dears for that adorable exclamation.

ABOUT HIS VOCAL TALENT

As a Dear (fan) for almost two years, while I cannot write his biography, I can share things I've learned about his singing by simply listening to him, his parents, grandparents, friends, etc. He's been interested in the concept of singing since he was a toddler. Singing was a staple like a food item around his home as well as musical instruments of all kinds. His favorite instrument? The dombra or a lute! He can play it in his sleep but he is very much awake when he shares some numbers with us at his concerts. A very exciting and highly anticipated part of his show is when he arrives in his culture's traditional male clothing with all kinds of bling and plays the dombra before he shares his favorite cultural songs.

I love the story, as all of his Dears do, about his refusing to go to kindergarten any longer if he couldn't also be studying in music classes too. What five-year old "threatens" boycotting school so he can attend **More School**?! Did he know something even then about his future? Don't know. Maybe his GA delivered some news to him too. The very involved paternal grandparents, especially his grandmother, saw to it that he attended those music classes for years. Dimash rarely misses an opportunity to thank her for those sacrifices. Dears love her for it too.

By the time he was six, he won first place in a contest with his peers in piano.

Wikipedia has up-to-date information on Dimash so I won't even try to enumerate his many accomplishments since he was six. Check it out. You'll be there for a while. What I do know or at least assume is that competition was a necessary evil and a blessing for many years. It helped him in so many ways to understand not only the music industry and the competitive vocal market but it encouraged him to practice more and more to get to singing levels that he wasn't hearing on the competitive scene. You have to stand out to be noticed. You have to have perfect pitch. And control??? Wow! That's imperative because vocal judges seem to be very impressed with control. They are so picky about it. It also helps a lot if you have more than a couple of octaves to claim. It helps a whole lot!

So fast-forward to the Chinese competition called "The Singer" in early 2017 and keep in mind how many multiple millions and millions could be watching him for the first time in China. (The latest I heard was 650,000,000 watched.) This 22 year old is invited as a wildcard, and its first foreigner at that, to participate with other singers from China. They are already popular or well known singers who are actually going to compete with each other and see what 500 audience members have to say after each performance with their judging credentials. I have no idea how many of those audience members were vocal experts but I do think they were vetted somehow. I believe the producers of the show and even Dimash thought he would be out of the competition in a matter of weeks. Surprise! Surprise!

Dimash, when it was all said and done, was the runner-up but oh so close. But that's not important and here's why. The morning following his first televised performance of S.O.S, he **needed** bodyguards. The only person in China who was shocked by that was Dimash Kudaibergen. How cute is that? This is when his life changed in so many ways. This was a before and after event. Life before the China competition and now life after. This is the part of "show business" that startles the novice or the newbie. Being recognized. It can be terrifying and gratifying at the same time. An interesting pairing of emotions. Dimash knows those emotions well now.

ABOUT THE MAN

How do you begin to write about a person you've never met but known all of your life? At least it feels that way sometimes. Some of my writings in this journal will give you some idea of how confusing it is to be so emotionally connected to a person that you've never met but feel like you know him better than your best friend. See the poem "I AM MUSIC" right after this introduction...... I think.

Dimash reveals so much about himself in interviews, backstage moments, interactions with fans, family, friends, fellow musicians and singers. He is a fan of many himself and his "fanboying" shows sometimes. He was "nervous" when he sang a few random songs with Bocelli at the piano (okay, Dimash, we will give you that one) and definitely smitten with the time he had with Lara Fabian (that one too). His collaboration with Russia's version of America's David Foster, **Igor Krutoy**, was **meant to be** and is now historical especially because Mr. Krutoy tabled his retirement years to work with Dimash. **In the cards**! I'm guessing that means Tarot cards. **Arranged by Allah!** They both have been fortunate and blessed not only to share their love for music in general but also to get to know each other, as Di said a few times, on a "father-son relationship" level. Igor is protective of Dimash and Dimash is respectful of him and grateful for his time and attention to his career. They have collaborated on many songs since 2019 and there should be many more to come. Dears love the Krutoy/Kudaibergen experiences. The K/K pairing is golden!

Dimash has revealed parts of his character and personality that paint a very pleasant picture. I'll start a list here but believe me I'll leave something out. Not on purpose but just because most of us can't think of everything. Here are some of the things he appears to be to me and his millions of fans. **Family oriented**. Family relationships are vital to him. Their support may be immeasurable. His gratitude is the same. **Friends** he trusts are essential to him. There are not much greater assurances in life but those guys and gals you can trust with your secrets or deepest feelings. **Fans/Dears.** As he has said many times "They are like family to me so I call them my Dears." **Children and Elders** get a great amount of attention and respect. Their happiness and joy are essential to him. **Peace on earth and healing the earth** are always a concern and he has done so much for those purposes but he is the last person who would want them enumerated. So I won't.

ABOUT THE WHOLE PACKAGE

When anyone is complimenting an entertainer by stating he/she has the whole package, we all know what that means, don't we? Later on, in one of my writings, I try to describe a disease his Dears have contracted because of our obsession with him. It goes like this… "**Dimashitosis** is the chronic incurable condition of a fan of Dimash Kudaibergen who has taken the obsession of his music, HIS LOOKS, his performance genius, HIS LOOKS, his humble personality, HIS LOOKS, and several other things, like HIS LOOKS, to such a level that she actually considers kidnapping. (Of course a Dear would never do that because I, uh, she looked it up and it's against the law, even in Kazakhstan. My, uh, her lawyer told me to include that part for legal reasons.)

So obviously, we need to discuss HIS LOOKS. Let's not skip THAT part. At twenty-six the man just slays you with his smile, his wink, his dad gum dimple, his hair (audible scream), his dark eyes that, okay, practically sees through your soul, his perfect lips (please don't make me elaborate on the lips) nose and jaw. Did I mention he's 6 ' 3" tall? That's a lot of Dimash Kudaibergen! I think that covers it. He's just tall, dark and handsome. That's all there is to it <u>but</u> once he sings accompanied by all that handsomeness and emotes all that emotion, he becomes gorgeous and hard to take. Dears joke and some are dead serious too about needing cold showers, ice from the freezer, a cold water splash to the face, a nice soft place to land when they faint and checking their pulses to see if they're still alive. It's a tough job but somebody's gotta do it.

Somebodies? No, allbodies have to look at him when he sings otherwise they are missing a nice percentage of their experience. Do you know that old recommendation when you are driving through a very small town and I mean a very small town and someone says "Don't blink or you may miss the whole town?" That's a recommendation for his concerts or his videos. Don't blink or you may miss that smile, that wink, that dimple that could hold a grape, those fingers as they synchronize with his voice as if they are telling him what notes to hit, hand gestures that foretell the upcoming note from that planet of his (DK ….phone home!) and those eyes that once again, penetrate your soul and discovers all of your secrets. Yep, you do not want to blink. His presence and charisma on stage won't let you *but* blink at your own risk. You've been warned. Fortunately, for him, and us we all enjoy that part of the experience. It's not only part of the experience but it completes **the whole package**. Wrapped up with a pretty red ribbon, some glitter and a flower or two….. or twelve.

ABOUT MY OBSESSION

My obsession began when I watched him for the first time on a CBS competition show in early winter of 2019. (SEE! The GA was right.) I believe it was February 10th to be exact. I have a love/hate relationship with that show, as do ALL of the Dears. We love it because it introduced many of us to Dimash. We hate it because they chose to treat him rather cruelly when he wanted to exit the show early to give the much younger competitors a shot at winning. What a guy! Dimash didn't need the "prize money" nor did he need the "winning title". Dimash knew he had **the win** and so did CBS but he couldn't accept it on the grounds that he simply could not win on the future careers of an 11 and 13 year old. A Kazakh cultural No-No. His treatment was unacceptable and we are shocked that they aired their tacky responses. But our humble Dimash came out of that situation much better off and we congratulate him for it. He will never, and never should, enter a competition again. He accomplished so much with those three performances including introducing a Kazakh singer to a large American audience. It was definitely a main objective of his.

The moment that first airing of him singing the popular French song, "S.O.S./An Earthly Being in Distress" was over, I was on YouTube checking this guy out like a fly on honey. Who is he? Where is he from? Kazakhstan? Where's that? How rare is it for any person to sing like that? Does he only sing French songs? Do Kazakhs speak French? How tall is he? How much does he weigh? What's his favorite food? Does he prefer mountains or beaches? After spending hours searching and listening and staring (I mean looking, of course) at him, the questions became a tad more serious. How does he get from wherever he is to Utah? How do I get from Utah to wherever he is? Will he sing for me at the drop of a hat? Or does he have to warm up? Will I have to pay him? Does it matter if I'm old enough to be his mother? Okay, grandmother! Will he leave his career so he can sit on the front porch with me and watch me get older? He can still sing but just to a smaller audience. These are important questions. But I had one problem. (Really Pam, just one?) I was still married to my husband of 49 years. So FINE! Moving on. Just concentrate on that voice and let it take you to other worlds.

AND IT DID!! Song after **amazing** (what a stupid word that doesn't work any more) song was a trip to places I've never heard of. You know, kind of like Kazakhstan. They say if you have a near death experience, an NDE, and go to heaven for a bit, when you return you can't use earthly words to describe the colors much less the sounds. That's our Dimash. When he's just singing in his middle registers, you would think he spent days fashioning or coloring each word. And you probably would be correct. Every octave, note, range, register, pitch, inflection, modulation, phonation, intonation (Don't be impressed with the list. I had to look those up.) and seventeen other musical phrases someone could list, are purposeful and intended. We feel it. We know it. WE LOVE IT!! Again, thank you Mr. Kudaibergen. We are always thanking him. He exists for **the love of music** and for the love that he has in **sharing that music. HE IS MUSIC!** Again, like NDE's, words cannot describe the colors of his notes much less the sounds coming out of his mouth. The surprises are everywhere. Most of the songs feel like they are going to be five minutes of slow low register ballads and then here comes the pole-vaulted head voice notes or operatic notes that clear the bar. I could go on and on about his vocal gymnastics. You can watch the best vocal coaches do that.

Over the last two years I have sacrificed, if you want to call it that, hours of television shows and movies for his videos. Poor Pammie. That leisure time took a back seat to hearing and consuming his videos like you would a hot pizza when you're starving or a tall glass of water when you're dehydrated. When life distracted me and I couldn't be watching/listening/devouring his videos, it was, well, a distraction like I said, but as soon as those dishes were done or that meal was cooked or the roof was shingled, I was back on the iPad and being fed musically, emotionally and spiritually. Ask any Dear and they'll identify. And by the way, I have never shingled a roof.

My Utah license plate is personalized and reads DIMASH1. The "1" part means "the No. 1 singer in the world" if anyone should ask. Above that license plate is a magnetic ad for his YouTube channel with his **perfect face** on it. I'm still waiting for the day that someone asks me "Who's the hunk on your trunk?" Can't wait!!! I just hope they are not in a hurry because they are going to get an earful and a slip of paper from my purse that says "All About Dimash Kudaibergen in 50 words or Less".

Seriously, I typed them up in the fall of 2019 and have been giving them out often to the Dimash-impaired population of Utah. See "Pam's Wondering…do you have Dimashitis" and you'll get the picture.

My other obsessive act (or rather a given) was to buy two tickets to his NY Arnau show for December 10, 2019, two plane tickets for me and that husband of mine who had no jealous bone in his body, thank goodness, and a hotel near the Barclays. Hello Helga! Hello Moldy Oldy! With no car obviously in NY, it was my first time to Uber.

Heck, it was my first time in NY and I've already **not** told you how old I am so that was a big deal too.

I was briefly in the acting business for about 4 minutes on stage in a play in Cedar City Utah (that's my professional picture for the play) and have performed my go-to-comedy skit for years. I've written roadshows and performed in some. I've judged drama and humorous competitions on a local, state and regional level for a year or so. I've watched and admired hundreds of actors and actresses but I had never wanted to go to New York to see a show or swoon over a celebrity. As a matter of fact I have lived for seven years in southern Utah-two hours away from Las Vegas-and do you know how many Celine Dion concerts I've seen? None. (Dimash probably KNOWS I'm crazy now.) And I think she's **amazing!** There's that word again.

BUT I HAD TO GET TO NEW YORK AND SEE DIMASH IN PERSON!! It would have been a regret I would not have wanted to live with. And if I didn't have the money at that time, I would have borrowed it from a rich relative or hit the streets. (Ooops, my Bishop could read that.) I've seen Elvis perform three times at the Monroe, Louisiana Civic Center but I lived 20 minutes away from that venue and never had to buy my ticket. Friends bought my ticket because I "stood in line for an hour." No real sacrifice to buy **our** tickets. No sacrifice whatsoever to see Mr. Presley. So do you get the picture?

How was the concert? HOW WAS THE CONCERT?!? **Unreal and otherwordly**. Dears use that word a lot. It was a dream come true and an out-of-body experience. Not exactly an NDE.....but close. The gal to my right when I asked said it was okay if I grabbed her arm or her leg when Dimash came out. I knew I was going to do something that I had no control over. Her knee received a major massage when he magically popped up out of that stage. I forgot to tell you he's a magician too. For a moment he was David Copperfield.

I'm watching and hearing Dimash Kudaibergen! What!? Yes, Pam, it's real. You are in New York City, the most famous city on the earth at the Barclays and you're watching his dream come true too. Why aren't you floating above your seat? I don't know. Gravity? So everybody's happy! Everybody's high on music and life. You spent some money and a few days in New York for your experience. Dimash prepared for this **for a decade**. It was an UNFORGETTABLE

DAY! An unforgettable cold and rainy week but I loved it and I would easily trade 100 Elvis concerts for one Dimash concert. No contest! Let's not even argue the point. And we won't belabor the fact that Elvis isn't touring anymore....at least not here.

Well, I think I heard somewhere that if you are writing facts about a person and you use more than 6,000 words that you are actually writing a biography. And since my Microsoft word thingy is telling me this is word #4860 and since I'm not intentionally writing his biography.... I better stop while I'm ahead.

ABOUT MY POETRY, SKITS, POSTINGS AND OTHER MUSINGS

My posts started several months back from the time of this printed journal and as long as the man does something different, like, I don't know, lick a flagpole, I am going to write a poem about it. It could be 20 stanzas long too. I don't know. I'll figure that out when the time comes. My mind has a mind of its own. But please Dimash....**do not lick a flagpole** especially during a Kazakh winter. Have you seen "A Christmas Story"?

He ate a pear while walking down the corridor of an airport. I wrote a poem about that. He held a large leaf in front of him for a photo shoot. I wrote a poem about that. He grew a beard for a couple of weeks and shared the pics and of course I wrote a poem about that. He "forgot" to wear a t-shirt for one of his IG posts and guess who wrote a poem about that? He's the cause of two well-known Dear diseases that I know of and I had to write about those. He had the audacity to be awesome and I wrote lots of poems about that. Somebody STOP me!!! On second thought...don't. Leave me alone. Thanks in advance.

Let me just say a few things about me that won't be in the *About the Author* part of this book. I have a few years behind me, way more than Dimash and way less than the oldest person alive on our planet but I have never been this *crazy* about another earthly human being besides really really close family members. It's an ENIGMA! I know that sounds like something you want your dermatologist to remove but it's not. And it's certainly not the other thing you're thinking. An enigma is a person or thing that is mysterious, puzzling or difficult to understand. Dimash is NOT the thing or person that is the enigma.

It is my **obsession** and millions of other Dears' obsession that is the enigma. Countless times I have read Dears' comments that only echo my situation. And they agree with me and Ms. Diana Ross that (insert musical notes) "If there's a cure for this, I don't want it. I don't want it. If there's a remedy, I'll run from it. I'll run from it." There's no pill or liquid we will swallow. No psychiatrist's couch on which we will recline. No clergy to which we will confess. No institution that could hold us captive inside with or without restraints as long as there's a Dimash Kudaibergen on the outside to hear and see. I'd take a bullet for the guy. But if I had a choice I would prefer taking that bullet in my left arm through the muscle and missing the bone. Yes, for sure missing the bone. That way I could say I took a bullet for Dimash Kudaibergen but I didn't die. That's always a good day.

The writings on the next whatever amount of pages to follow (because there may be a dozen new poems inside of me yet to write, especially if he licks that flagpole) will serve to express other feelings and observations I have and like I said, millions of other Dears, have about Di, Dimash, Mr. Kudaibergen, Dimash Kudaibergen, Mr. Qudaibergen, Dinmukhammed Kanatuly Kudaibergen to be exact, I think. Can you think you're exact? And some of my writings will express his sentiments about fame too.

I'm signing off here and will add the musings now and hope that if God allows Mr. DKKQ to read these one day, that he will at least be amused with this Dear of his and her journal. After all you made me a Dear. You're responsible. I never asked for this and you may have some 'splainin' to do. The jury's still out.

Good night Mr. K(Q)udaibergen and pleasant dreams while visions of musical notes dance in your head. Nope. That may keep you awake so never mind. Get your usual four hours of restful sleep and then go to work in your magically mysterious musical laboratory and create, create, create, Mr. I AM MUSIC.

And I thank YOU in advance.

PAMELA MCGEE WILKINSON

P.S. to Dimash

Please do not let any of these complimentary statements go to your head. After all you are just a regular guy from Kazakhstan who just happens to sing well. If you do let that happen and start getting "all full of yourself", I'm sure Mama Miua will, to use a Southern American term, "Slap you upside the head!" Just sayin'.

P.S. to non-Dears

If you are not a dear yet and want to know how to start learning about and listening to Dimash, always go to his YouTube channel first. Eat those songs up for breakfast, lunch and dinner, and then head to other channels. WHEN you become "hooked", mark it on your calendar. You'll want to celebrate that day every year. You're welcome.

25 January 2021

I AM MUSIC - THE POEM

Someone once wrote: "Not everything that counts can be counted, and not everything that can be counted....counts."

I AM MUSIC

By Pamela McGee Wilkinson (and comments from Dears in quotations)

> If you believe in life before life
> Then we will have a good place to start
> I believe we lived as a spirit being
> Before we got a body and a heart.
>
> If life before life is truly a truth
> Then maybe that will explain
> Why you meet someone you've always known
> But it's the first time you've uttered their name.
>
> It's the first time you've seen their face or their frame
> It's the first time you spoke and conversed
> Yet you know this person much too well
> Though it's the first time you have met on earth.
>
> This acquaintance strikes an interesting chord
> And it resonates through your heart and your mind

That this person's true connection to you
is not of the earthly kind.

If what I have said here at the beginning
May not be abundantly clear
It may be a legitimate way
To explain why we've all become Dears.

Our first reaction to this guy named Dimash
Was like a comfortable slap on your face
It wakes you up and proves you're alive
But puts you in a very strange place.

You've never ever been there before
The landscape and air is rarefied
But you'll always want to stay there
If this man can stay by your side.

And he always will be by your side
As he lifts your heart with his songs.
He's created a vehicle for singing
And he wants to bring you along.

Music that escapes his mouth
Is like a bird on a gossamer wing
Flying through the air to reach a star
Or other Heavenly things.

Mr. Kudaibergen IS the MUSIC
And he's constantly seeking perfection
As a tribute to his Holy Creator
And to seek His approval and direction.

The MUSIC is searching to find that home
Where the MUSIC was actually created
He wants to thank the Creator of it all
And his gratitude can't be overstated.

As we spend some time with MUSIC
We try to explain our loss
For words that actually can describe
Our feelings for Mr. Dimash.

We Dears have spoken and spoken well
But with earthly words that betray
They can't come close to testifying
Or mean what we're trying to say.

"His voice is the voice of many angels."
"His magic" "His smile" "His soul catching eyes".
"Dimash is hope and light in my life."
And he's all that heaven implies.

"I love you Di, today, tomorrow and forever"
"I love him like salt" that is essential to me
I love his "integrity". And his "authenticity".
For "his respect for traditions and country".

"The movement of his hands while he sings".
"His voice, unique and incomparable".
"I want you to be my song from the beginning to the end".
A day without his voice is intolerable.

So back to the beginning and that familiar impression
An impression you want to explore.
Perhaps Dimash was our friend in heaven
And he is music NOW as he was BEFORE.

He came to earth at the perfect time
Our souls have been musically kissed
He gives his songs humbly and freely
And chose them from a heavenly list.

So Dears....your sentiments helped write this poem
We did our best with earthly speech
And we agree that MUSIC came here
To sing and to love and to teach.

We earthly beings in distress
Need not write S.O.S. in the sands
But just stop and listen to MUSIC
Then we'll be in his capable hands.

Dimash is a reluctant singing star
He doesn't like the trappings of fame.
He's uncomfortable with the notion of celebrity
But he accepts it just the same.

He insists he's just a regular guy
That happens to know how to sing
That anything else we label him with
Is a very uncomfortable thing.

Prince Dimash! The Best Voice on Earth!
Okay....those labels should do
But YOU are so much more to us
Than the sounds that come out of you.

December 19, 2020

DIMASH QUDAIBERGEN

A singer by any other name
Would definitely not sing as sweet
Nor would he command the stage as well
Or have the world at his feet.

Nor would he reach an octave
That can send your heart to space
Or make you forget your every care
While just gazing upon his face.

For he is a travelling poet
And stops to sing along the way
As he gathers lyrics and musical notes
And adds them to his bouquet.

A literal bouquet of musical things
That define this singer's art

And he's proven time and time again
That his bouquet starts with his heart.

The bouquet's foundation is a heart full of love
It's a testament of caring
And as the singer has said in many ways
His gift from God is for sharing.

And while HE gathers bouquets of flowers
At the end of each musical show
He wants us to know that they are symbolic
Of the bouquet he wants to bestow.

He gives a bouquet to each of us
But we hold it in our hearts not our hands
And he's confident it's not enough of a gift
To thank his many fans.

So Dimash....

While roses are still red
And violets are still blue
The author who wrote that sonnet
Had never ever met you.

For he would have written a novel
To name all the flowers you bring
When you stand upon a theater's stage
And open your heart and sing.

Pamela Wilkinson
27 January 2021

THE RECEIVING PLACE

All of us need a place to land
When life is too much to take
We need to find a chance to breathe
And expel the worldly waste.

We need the act of rejuvenation
We need the power of cleanse
Like peeling off your dirty socks
Or exhaling while counting to ten.

So if you've ever counted to ten
Or peeled off those "dirty socks"
Where do you go for that needed rest
Do you nap or sit on a rock?

I knew a lady a long while back
Who was the mother of nine
Who sat on a boulder outside her home
And had a lovely time.

She took deep breaths and pushed them out
To the let world have a turn
And learned that healing while on her rock
Was a very nice way to learn

That life offers good and bad
and Everything in between
But daily struggles sharpen our minds
And keep our engines clean.

Not everyone has a boulder
They can call their healing place
Where they receive that rejuvenation
And expel the worldly waste.

But I know of millions of people
From countries too many to name
Who've found the receiving place
And their locus is all the same.

They find it interestingly enough
From a man of considered fame
Whose voice is literally out of this world
And Qudaibergen is his name.

He's famous for taking you places
That most men have never known
He lifts your hearts and massages them
With gentle AND powerful tones.

His whispers while singing are deafening
And that sounds like a dichotomy
But you'd have to listen to understand
How that contrast can come to be.

His gentle angelic whispering tones
Pull you into his head and heart
And just when you've settled into that heavenly realm
There are vocals that are off the charts.

It's hard to describe this phenomenon
Better than me have also tried
But generally we all become speechless
As the words we use can't describe

The reaction of hearing a perfect voice
Coming from his handsome face
And knowing that from this moment and from now on
He will be our receiving place.

24 January 2021

A MAGNIFICENT OBSESSION - preface

Dears

I fell asleep in my comfortable chair for maybe an hour or two last night and woke to these words in my head: "The mood is set to glorious". And I knew instantly what it meant. I don't hesitate when that happens. I know what to do. Get the iphone notebook out and start poeming. Yep, poeming, because it seems to be my pastime and I might as well use it as the verb it can be. So, I'll let it be. As I dictated "The mood is set to glorious" then came "The lighting is just right" and the rest of the poeming is history for me.

But I discovered after a few stanzas that the theme of this poem wasn't about me or dears in my situation but it was about the hard-working gals out there who come home exhausted and spent and ready to relax and unwind in a way that has become an enigma to her and thousands and thousands and thousands (millions, then) of others who walk in her shoes. God bless you for all you do to make the world outside your home better. You deserve your time with Dimash and the magical way he turns your heavy heart into a lighter sense of self and sends you off to a place that has nothing to do with giving and giving but receiving and receiving.

A MAGNIFICENT OBSESSION

The mood is set to glorious
The lighting is just right
Her glass is full and her heart is ready
To hear his songs tonight.

Her day was long and tedious
She's given it all she can
She worked her tiny miracles
But now it's time for "the man".

The Music Man, The Man of Song
The Giver of His Gifts
The one, No wait! The only One
Who makes her axis shift.

She settles in for a magical night
As she turns the world away
She readies herself, she braces herself
For the genius on display.

She's searching for the very first song
that sent her to the moon
She needs to hear those tones again
She needs to hear them soon.

She needs to return to that special place
She visited years before
When S.O.S. broke her heart
And sent it to the floor.

She needs this respite this time of night
As the daylight required too much
She needs, No Wait! She really deserves
The singer's magic touch.

But wait, hold on for a just a sec
Is it Sinful Passion she requires?
Those powerful notes that shocked her soul
When she listened for hours and hours.

This earthly being and her stress
Is about to be contained
By this walking, singing miracle
Who cannot be explained.

She contemplates the next song to play
Will it be Love is Like a Dream?
Or can she handle Daybreak
And its heartbreaking familial theme?

The sessions she plans with this singer
Has a start, a middle and an end
As sleep soon overpowers her core
And the routine begins again.

For tomorrow will be another day
She will, of course, give it her best
But she'll come home to another splendid chance
To put her heart at rest.

She never understands the hold
This strangest sense of possession
And why this singer changed her life
And became a magnificent obsession.

January 23, 2021

THERE'S SOMETHING WRONG WITH HIM!

Hey!! Do you see that guy? Yes...that guy!

Well there's something seriously wrong with him.

I honestly don't know exactly what it is right now but there has to be something seriously wrong with him. And I've got to figure it out.

For two years I've been searching and resourcing and sleuthing but I haven't found anything yet that I can call him on.

I've been SPECULATING a lot about what could be wrong with him like…

Maybe he doesn't take his dishes to the sink.

Or maybe he forgets to put the toilet seat down for the ladies in the house (Come on ladies ..most men don't)

Or maybe he lies about his weight or his age.

Maybe when some gal asks him " Do I look fat in this?" He says "No. It's actually very slimming" but he won't look her in the eye when he says it.

Maybe when he's out to lunch with friends and when they're not looking he steals the last bite off of their plate and blames it on someone else.

Or maybe he's forgetful because …it wasn't that long ago that I posted that my birthday was on January 18th and that I liked Ghirardelli chocolates and yellow roses. And guess who didn't get Ghirardelli chocolates and yellow roses on her birthday? Yes…. ME!! Not a thing from Dimash Kudaibergen!

Or maybe he cuts in line at the local KFC and excuses himself with the sorry excuse that "I'm a famous celebrity and my time is valuable and I really need some crispy chicken!" Geez Dimash!

Or maybe sometimes he gets really lazy and forgets to shave.

Or maybe he's one of those people who keeps promising that he'll do something and then he never does.

Or maybe he's one of those people who always forgets to bring his wallet so that others can pay for the meal.

Or maybe he sometimes forgets to wear socks.

Or maybe sometimes he's walking around in an airport eating a pear in front of a bunch of people and doesn't offer them one.

Or maybe he.....

Oh forget it Pam. You already know what's wrong with him. And it's something that usually drives the rest of us crazy... and generally.... because it's just not fair.

That guy down there....yes that guy....

Well.....HE'S PERFECT!!!   19 JANUARY 2021

DIGITAL DIMASH MAGIC

Just when you think it's safe to relax
And that everything is the same
Dimash Qudaibergen and his Dream Team
Literally ELEVATE their game.

These musical geniuses
The singers, choreographers and crew
Came up with a plan to astonish us
With something fresh, amazing and new.

The technical gymnastics
And Dimash's passionate songs
Weave a magical carpet ride
And they take us all along.

We are holding on for Dear life
We're subjected to jolts and spurts
We've waited and waited and waited for this
And boy did that ever hurt!

But now we've seen melodious results
Waiting was definitely "worth the wait"
The Dream Team gave us an hour and a half
And it started right out of the gate.

Olimpico is beautifully launched
from a very nice creamy sofa
And Dimash is singing it perfectly
And he looks like Casanova.

Then here comes Give Me Your Love
His very own composition
But who invited the pretty brunette?
Just who made that decision?

Words cannot describe the Dears' total satisfaction
Their joy is ALL over the net
And the whole ENTIRE digital experience
is something we will never forget.

From the perfect beginning
to the very surprising end
The dears will be talking about this
Again and again and again!!

And now that we know relaxing isn't safe
And nothing will be the same
Dimash Qudaibergen and his Dream Team
Just elevated their FAME!

Thank You Di and your Dream Team

HARD WORK NOTED AND APPRECIATED!!!

Pam of Utah
17 January 2021

THE LETHAL WEAPON

Since no picture is available for this poem, I will attempt to describe it. Dimash and Kanat are apparently just getting off of a flight and headed toward the Dears. Kanat is about eight steps ahead of him but blocking some of the view of our Dimash who looks dapper (that's an ancient word but he sure looks DAPPER!) in a black suit and awesome sunglasses and he looks about 7 ft tall. Mr. Kanat has a big smile on his face. I'm sure most of the Dears have seen this airport photo. Check your Dimash picture album on your phone. It's probably in there.

THE LETHAL WEAPON By Pamela McGee Wilkinson

Excuse me, Mr. Kanat
But you're kinda in our way.
You're kinda blocking our view right now
And you may just ruin our day.
We came to this airport to see your son
We've been waiting since 4 A.M.
We may not get to shake his hand
But we sure want to LOOK at him.

It's your entire fault you know
Yours and your wife, Sveta
Producing an amazing man like that
You really should've known bveta. (Not a typo)
And planting that darn DNA in him
That formed his vocal folds
Was really a nasty trick of yours
If the truth be really told.
So the man inherited all your talents
And his mother's talents too
And then you let him borrow your looks
PARENTS, what's wrong with you?
You produced this dangerous lethal weapon
Who's traveling all over the place
Walking around at 6 foot 3
And sporting a killer face.
We see you smiling at the crowd
Thinking "Yes Dears ….Look what I did.
I'm the father of this lethal weapon
I'm his Dad and he's MY kid!"
We can see that you're a very proud Dad
We can read that in your grin.
But my goodness, Sir! What did you do?
We can't get enough of him!
We can't get enough of his stellar voice
We can't get enough of his looks
So can you please just step aside for a sec
Before you get smacked with a book!
Oh Mr. Kanat, we say that in jest
We're kidding! We're kidding, for sure!
But what do you expect from Dears with a disease
When Dimash is the only cure?
Oh look! Kanat just moved aside
And Dimash is standing right HERE!
He's reaching out to touch our hands
He HUGGED that lucky Dear!
He's taking our flowers and thanking us
The man is precious to boot
We can't believe how tall he is
And thank you for wearing that suit!
A precious few minutes have sadly passed

We've seen Dimash. Touched his hand.
But now it's time for him and his Dad
To return to their motherland.
Goodbye Mr. Kudaibergen. Goodbye Mr. Aitbayev.
Thanks for spending this time with us.
You've got a departing plane to catch
And we've got to get on the bus.
So go your way and we'll go ours
These memories won't disappear
We'll never forget our time with him
or our day in the life of a Dear.

January 6, 2021

Based on what most horse enthusiasts feel about their favorite horse, I wrote this from Di's possible perspective. Surely when he returns to his home in Kazakhstan, he must look forward to an afternoon riding his horse. The title assumes that he needs to escape fully from time to time from the hustle and bustle of the entertainment world. Nature plus a beautiful horse must equal repair for our Dimash.

THE MASTER'S REPAIR
BY PAMELA MCGEE WILKINSON

As soon as the master approaches this horse
His mind begins to relax
He shelves the worries and business of life
The details, commitments and facts.

He mounts the horse and it's very clear
That the master is in command
He remembers the gait the master prefers
He knows the vistas and land.

He knows the paths that he must take
To aid in the master's repair
He finds the lake and a grove of trees
They find tranquility there.

They travel and travel down beaten paths
They stop and rest by a brook
The horse finds a flourishing apple tree
The master reads a good book.

There's a time and season for all things
There's a time for reparation
Di takes advantage of hours like these
And enjoys the anticipation.

There's a psychic connection between the two
They share their life's ups and downs
They treasure their precious time together
Their gratitude has no bounds.

As dusk begins to show her face
And the sun begins to set
The master mounts his horse again
With a certain sense of regret.

It's time to return to that other world
Where commitments and rules have their way
He returns to his barn and he returns to his house
At the end of this peaceful day.

1 JANUARY 2021

THE DIMASH SMILE

If Rembrandt needed an agreeable muse
Just to paint a noble face
He wouldn't have to look very far indeed
To cover his canvas space.

What a smile does to our singer's countenance
Should be rightly considered illegal
Some smiles are cute and very childlike
And some are simply regal.

There are certain smiles that last for days
There are some that are quick but sweet

There are some when he's singing to us Dears
That could bring us to our feet.

There are some that say he is satisfied
There are some that sound an alarm
There are some that whisper "I love you Dears"
There are some that reveal his charm.

There are some that show his lighter side
There are some that expose his thoughts
There are some that are quite mysterious
And hide all the secrets he's got.

Some smiles invite you to c'mon in
The weather is fine in here
I'm happy and content with my life right now
I want to share it with all of my Dears.

The Dears can hardly stand them
Those smiles always seem to deliver
They send us to the moon and back
They make us melt or simply shiver.

His smiles are part of the proverbial package
Along with his talent and grace
They add an extra special touch
To the canvas that is his FACE.
To the man of many smiles.....
Pamela McGee Wilkinson JANUARY 1, 2021

THE GIFT THAT KEEPS ON GIVING

DEARS........On Christmas Eve I received a scarf with an image of Dimash on the front. I will always have it and appreciate it but it wasn't just a gift for that day. It is a gift for every day and that reality is what inspired this poem. A poem of gratitude that we all feel. Pam

THE GIFT THAT KEEPS ON GIVING.
By Pamela McGee Wilkinson

If Dimash Kudaibergen is a Gift from God
Who delivers his songs for a living
Then shouldn't he, in the end, be called
The Gift that keeps on giving?

And who doesn't like receiving a gift
That lasts for years, is enchanted
That means it is never lost or wasted
or never taken for granted.

We've all received gifts that are gone in a day
That spoil or aren't worth their cost
That maybe lose their intrinsic value
Are misplaced or eventually lost.

But not so....this Gifted Singer
We received this Gift with aplomb
That he will keep on giving and giving
From now and till kingdom come.

He offers us often a musical present
That's wrapped in an amber bow
With ribbons of silvery satin and lace
And decorative elements for show.

Each song is worth its weight in gilt
For the effort required is untold
But still it's offered on a silver platter
As a precious rose of gold.

This Giver of gifts is pleased beyond measure
He delights in being the Giver
And as we accept each offer of song
We become the thankful receiver.

There are composers to bless for the music
And lyricists who fashion the language
When our singer delivers HIS vocal prizes
He completes this musical package.

Thank you Dimash Kudaibergen
We hear you with souls that are open
Our admiration for you cannot be measured
But we give you our hearts as a token.

Pam of Utah
27 December 2020

A CHRISTMAS SCARF
By Pamela McGee Wilkinson

Dimash just THINKS
he is in Kazakhstan
Enjoying family and friends
Working in his studio
until the evening ends.

Dimash just THINKS
he's resting comfortably
In his favorite TV chair
Searching for that video
When he had longer hair.

Dimash just THINKS
while eating a sirloin steak
With seasoned curly fries
that everything is certain and real
In front of his very eyes.

But he would be mistaken
Oh yes he would be wrong
Because the fact is
he's been here
In Utah all along.

(Hey!! A gal can dream.)

Thanks friends Terri and Paul
For the best present ever.

Pam of Utah
24 December 2020

This is a chair in my living room with my Christmas scarf draped over it. This is where he lives in my house. Pam

THE PHOTO REVISITED

(Or lovingly referred to as the Fruitful Day Photo)
(Because....oh well, why not?)

Dimash was working hard that day
He says it was very fruitful
So naturally he got his cell phone out
and gave us all an eyeful. (Eyeful definition: A visually striking person or thing....Yep)

We guess it's not a routine thing
He's done this only once before
We won't be the first and we won't be the last
To say… we're okay with more.

Maybe it could be a yearly post
Like a yearly birthday gift
Just a gesture to thank all the dears
And give those gals a lift.

"I'll prove to them with yearly posts
That it wasn't just a prank.
After all they do so much for me
And I have them all to thank."

"So if lying in bed without a shirt
Can muster up a stir
I guess I should repeat this scene
And give the gals some more."

"History can repeat itself
Sometimes we learn a lot
But I'll never understand the fuss there was
Because of the shoulders I've got."

That really was so nice of you
You're such a sport to share
We'll take all of your intriguing pics
If you've got some more to spare.

"Oh! The dears are awfully cute and sweet
And their comments are delightful
But they may have to wait a few more months
Before another eyeful."

The End.
The Sad End.
December 22, 2020

BREAKING THE NEWS TO MOM

*About the Fruitful Day Photo

DIMASH: (enters the kitchen with an actual t-shirt on and a big smile on his face and says)
Hey mom! Look what I just sent to my dears.

(shows shirtless selfie to Sveta) (say that 3 times really fast)

SVETA: (eyes big and jaw dropped)
Dimash! You're going to drive them crazy!!!

DIMASH: OK. And what's your point?

(Dimash grabs a pear from the fruit bowl and leaves the kitchen for his sexy bedroom)

AND THE REST IS HISTORY

*(I DARE SOME DEAR TO ACT OUT THIS SCENE AND POST IT ON YOUR FAN PAGE -
BORROW YOUR SON OR YOUR GRANDSON AND MAKE HIM DIMASH FOR A DAY)

ASTROLATRY

Astrolatry is ruining my life
And I caught it a little while back
It keeps me busy that's for sure
But it reminds me of things that I lack.

Like reading more great or classic books
or working on genealogy
But I can't seem to get to those noble things
Because of ASTROLATRY!

Actually though…it's not such a burden
At least it can fill up the days
It keeps my idle mind busy busy busy
In some most unusual ways.

Sometimes I'm looking up pictures
And sometimes I am watching a film
Sometimes I'm writing poetry
Because I'm thinking of HIM.

Oh dear, I think I just revealed a clue
But now I'll give you some more
The focus of my astrolatry
Is some guy YOU also adore.

He sings like an angel from heaven above
And is as tall as your living room door
He's very, very pleasing to the eyes
And is humble to his absolute core.

Have I given you now just enough hints
And have you guessed what astrolatry is?
Have you figured out the meaning of IT
By reading through all of this?

Astrolatry in case you are clueless
And haven't yet looked it up
Is the worship of celestial bodies
Like planets and STARS and stuff.

Well, worship may be too strong a word
It depends on your perspective
Use any description you wish or please
If that is your objective.

However you want to define
Your case of astrolatry
As long as it works for you and them
I guess it will work for me.

So now we have to face it
Our life with DIMASH is a "fix".
He's like a habit you just can't kick
This young man of twenty-six.

He keeps singing us to a special place
That doesn't exist on earth
They say he's been refining his voice
A short time after his birth.

SO.....I guess we'll all have to admit
That it's not such a very bad thing
To focus some of our leisure time
On this STAR who KNOWS how to sing!

Thanks Dimash!
You are definitely THE MAN !!!

Pam of Utah
December 17, 2020

PAM WONDERS.......IS DIMASH OUR MUSE?

And she's also wondering how you can compare Dimash to Santa Claus. Well, just give me a New York minute and I'll figure it out.

Muse: A person or personified force that is the source of inspiration for a creative artist.

Dears, have you been paying attention to the many dears who feel inspired by Dimash Kudaibergen's talent and channel that inspiration into some creativity of their own. Not that they want to be world-famous like he is but they do have a desire to find a talent or resurrect one.

Some have taken up their painting or drawings again. Some are getting back to the piano or their violins. Some have called up their former vocal coaches and said, "I'm ready to work on my singing again". And some like myself have resurrected their love for many forms of writing.

This particular consequence of following Dimash Kudaibergen is very interesting to me and a confirmation of the science of inspiration. If there is such a thing. Yes, let's just say that inspiration can be a science.

The thing about inspiration is that it hits you whenever it wants to as if it has a mind of its own. I recently posted a poem called The Sculptor. My reading that morning of several dears' comments as they tried to explain WHO Dimash Kudaibergen is and how did he get that way inspired that poem? All at once, there was an image of a sculptor at work trying to sculpt a Dimash Kudaibergen. More about this poem and its provenance is included below in a reply to a comment from a fellow Utah dear who was curious about how long it took to write 31 stanzas. But hang on because the Part II of The Sculptor has 57 stanzas.

I have been inspired by Dimash's beard, his pear and his giant leaf. A poem that I wrote 20 years ago and decided to self publish a few months ago was inspired by a postcard and the voice of my first granddaughter who turned her American accent into a British one while she and her parents were living in England for a while. In an instant she was an English princess and the poem was born. I couldn't get pen and paper in my hand fast enough.

The voice of inspiration can be very demanding and insist you put everything down until the creation process is over. (Pay attention to my last sentence below. That's where you come in.)

Krissy

I know exactly when I started and I know exactly when I finished writing this poem. But I am kind of a perfectionist so I check it and edit it over and over and over again for errors or wait for additional stanzas. As a matter of fact, I just noticed an error and edited it five minutes ago. But I'd rather not reveal how long it took. I'll keep it a secret for now. But I love getting inspired by something and the story starts unfolding in my head and I can't get to my notebook app fast enough. It's such a joy to make them happen but a burden to keep them from being corny or cheesy. I'm sure I'm guilty of corny and cheesy but, oh well.

In a way this is my "Twas the Night Before Christmas". The author of that Christmas classic wakes up and discovers Santa. But the sculptor in this fable wakes up to see what he has created. In a way, don't we think that Dimash has a fantastical quality like Santa? Santa arrives with his eight magical reindeer and delivers his "presents". Dimash arrives with his eight magical octaves and delivers his "presence". Both of those larger than life men are our fantasies and we are sometimes living in their world riding with them in their conveyances....Santa's sleigh and Di's spaceship. Fun times.

So what Pam is wondering is… How has Dimash been your muse? And it doesn't have to be an art that was revisited. There are many other ways that he has or can inspire. Many!

Thanks Dears for indulging my musings on our Muse.

Pam of Utah
12 December 2020

This was a fairly popular post as many Dears had stories to tell of his influence on their creative juices and how some of those juices had been rejuvenated. I have heard those stories numerous times in others' posts. Many Dears explained other ways he has inspired them.

THE CHOIR IS HERE!

8 December 2020

Scene: A large stage with a stadium like platform for many singers.

Substitute Choir Director to Event Producer:

Director: "Hello. Well, I'm here. I'm your replacement Director. Sorry about the other guy. I hope he feels better sooner than later. So what's going on? I hear it's a songfest rehearsal of some kind."

Producer: "Well not exactly. It is a festival and there will be a lot of songs. The choir hasn't arrived yet. Running a bit late. The choir has just left a charity event nearby."

Director: "Oh! Well that was nice of them. So how many choir members are we looking for and how many cameras have we set up?"

Producer: "Just one camera but there will be roughly 10 to 12 voices."

Director: "So 10 to 12 choir members but only one camera? How are we going to get a tight shot on 10 to 12 singers?"

Producer: "Oh, we will get a tight shot all right. Don't worry about that."

Director: "I don't understand. Are you trying to be evasive? How is one camera going to cover 10 to 12 singers?"

Producer: "The choir has always needed just one camera at these festivals. It will work out fine. You'll see. Oh, here comes the choir now."

Director: "I just see that one tall guy. Where is the rest of the choir?"

Producer: **"He IS the choir!"**

Director: (Jaw drop)

Producer: "Hi Dimash.

Dimash: Hello.

The End (except the new Choir Director ordered the unnecessary stadium platform to be removed)

In conjunction with the now age-old question for Dimash....

Any Choir Director: "So Dimash, the next number needs a tenor, a bass, an alto and a soprano. Which one would you prefer today?"

Dimash: "Yes"

THE SCULPTOR

Dears   December 10, 2020

For many of us, this day is the day that will live in infamy. I was there as many of you were when we were privileged to see and hear Dimash Kudaibergen at the Barclays in New York. This post isn't about that night but if it weren't for what happened below, he would never have made it to the Barclays or anywhere else for that matter. We all know how Dimash came to be (we really are not stupid) and we are still trying to convince ourselves that he didn't come from another planet. But what if.......

> I'll bet that you are special
> I am too so I've been told
> But Dimash Kudaibergen? Well, let me tell you
> he broke that "special" mold.
>
> The following is a fable
> of how he came to be
> For when he was created
> He was different than you and me.
>
> For to create means "to organize"
> You begin with thoughts and ideas
> and then you add materials
> and see what the end result is.
>
> The Sculptor in this creation story
> saw a vision late one eve
> And quickly tumbled out of bed
> To roll up his Sculptor's sleeve.

He examined his usual shelves of molds
that he used almost every day
But scratched his head and grit his teeth
and said "Gee! There's just no way!"

(Now, let's hear the Sculptor's story in his own words)

The vision of that man I saw
Should not come from these average molds
For these are rather common and plain
if the truth be really told.

I wondered, now whispering to myself
There are some rare molds up there.
Some I've never ever used before
And some I'd never ever share.

I'll have to grab my ladder
for that shelf is way too high
I'm glad I've never used these molds
For now I think I know why.

You see, I bought them long ago
from a man who was sublime
At crafting molds of faces and hands
and bodies of every kind.

I remember now that he told me
that I'm buying the only set
That when and if I use them
That I'm never ever to forget

That he'd never had a vision
or a model that would suffice
To use these molds for just anyone
Because they're really, really nice.

"I'm not trying to be boastful, he said
About my talent or my skill
I'm just trying to convey this thought to you
Before you settle the bill.....

That these molds could one day be priceless
Or you may have to throw them away
After you create Your Creation
That's all I am trying to say."

So I paid the gentleman what I owed
And stored the molds away
And said "For now, I'm thinking
I'll just put them on display."

But that was many many years ago
around Nineteen Ninety Four
I think it was May the 24th
If anyone's keeping score.

(So the Sculptor went to work that day
With these molds he dusted off
And when he saw what he had created
He stammered and choked and coughed.)

What have I created now?!
Is this really the vision I saw?
Look at those eyes and those perfect lips
That nose, that majestic jaw.

Those hands and fingers look so strong
I know they'll serve him well
He will use them for many, many wonderful things
But for what I could never tell.

What is this art I've created?
He's such a beautiful sight.
His visage is simply ethereal
But how about that height?

He's standing 6 foot 3 inches tall
That's taller than me and my brothers
His shoulders are wide, his waist is small
He's just not like all the others.

I think I'll give him raven hair
And lots of it to boot
And when it is combed and styled just right
He'll look handsome in any suit.

But something else is going on
He's more than a figure with hair
There's something shining from his face
That makes we want to stare.

It's as if a passion for the spice of life
Is screaming to come out
I'll bet he will be an artist of some sort
Yes. That's what that's all about.

But at the same time when you see his face
There's a light that you will find
There's the power of love and compassion
For all of humankind.

Oh my goodness! What am I making?
This truly is surreal
I've never sculpted something like him
He's so powerful but so very still.

I'm afraid to send him out to the world
His essence is so very strong
He's really not meant to be on this earth
But that's where he belongs.

Who knows what this man will become
If he makes all the right choices
And follows a more than average path
And listens to all the right voices.

And even though I see his humanness
He's more than that I'm afraid
The world will be aware of that
When they hear the statements he's made.

So now I have these molds to consider
Should I destroy them or put them away
Or should I sell them to the highest bidder
And just go about my day.

Nope. I'll never ever use them again
And no, they won't be sold
Because this man I've created today
Deserves his own special mold.

Oh, he will set out to conquer the world
And his heart will be on display
And your first look at this earthly Prince
Will be an unforgettable day.

Pam of Utah
10 December 2020

(in loving memory of our December 10th Arnau New York experience) and now The Sculptors Masterpiece or Part II of The Sculptor

THE SCULPTOR'S MASTERPIECE

Our sculptor continued to stare and stare
At this man that he created.
He was captivated by his very essence
He was visibly elated.

He paced and paced in his studio.
He tossed his glasses and exclaimed.
Will someone please tell me what's going on?
Is there someone out there to blame?

I've never had this feeling before
That I was not the creator.
I feel I'm just the conduit
For something surely greater.

I don't remember when I started
I barely remember the finish.
Was I actually physically here all along?
Oh My! Now I'm just sounding foolish.

Of course I was here and very present.
I remember the hours I spent.
I remember the clay staining my hands
And I remember the feel and the scent.

But my hands seemed to move on their very own
As if I had no command.
They shaped, they formed, they fashioned.
They knew how to make this man.

It was abnormal and very dreamlike
The smell and the feel and the texture.
Was the clay as unusual as the molds?
Or is that just my conjecture?

Do I now understand what the crafter meant
When he said these molds are special.
He even used the "priceless" word
As if he meant "consequential".

I'm having confusing feelings now
To explain these moments in time
When I worked today in this studio
And entered the world of sublime.

So here I stand perplexed as can be.
The answers aren't coming forth.
But there is one thing that is certain to me.
This man has significant worth.

As of now he's just a statue of clay
That happens to be surreal.
I ceremoniously put the molds away
But what is this mystical feel?

The sculptor had to exit the scene.
He was bewildered and overcome.
He knew not what to do with this man
But he surmised what he would become.

I have to take a much-needed break
This problem is getting to me.
I need a beautiful but simple distraction
But what could that distraction be?

Oh yes! I'll play some classical music
Like Beethoven, Stravinsky or Bach.
(He contemplated which composer to choose
While removing his sculptor's smock.)

I believe a sonata from Beethoven
Would certainly rest my heart.
I'll play the album that I just bought
That sounds like an excellent start.

He prepared a tea with some honey and lemon
And sat down in his favorite chair.
He closed his eyes and leaned way back
As the music filled the air.

He quickly and gracefully fell asleep
But his teacup crashed to the floor.
He awakened and thought to clean it up
But sleep….he wanted more.

He settled again into a sweet, sweet slumber
He needed the rest you see
For having a part of the creation that day
Made him tired and drained and weary.

As he napped and entered a dreamy state
The music's volume seemed to grow.
He didn't make a move at first
But he surely wanted to know.

Why WAS the music getting louder?
Was the player beginning to fail?
He finally opened his eyes a bit
And noticed a handsome male.

He was tall and very dignified
His presence filled the space.
The sculptor rubbed his eyes three times
Then recognized his face.

You're my creation! he said aloud
But you've surely come to life.
What made this happen? Why are you here?
I must go get my wife!

No! Please don't do that. I'll explain.
You can tell her another time.
I am the creation that you helped form
And my form is in its prime.

When you purchased and stored those special molds
It was me that you actually bought.
The crafter was trying to explain it to you
But you couldn't read his thoughts.

He never tried to form me
As he knew it couldn't be done.
He needed a very special artist
And he knew that you were the one.

Oh, there were other attempts to buy my molds.
There were others who wanted to try.
But he kindly and politely sent them away
Until you came …by and by.

But what you and I can't explain
And may never really understand.
Is that I was waiting for this very day
To be formed by your special hands.

Your human traits, your artistic talent
Was just the help I required
To become the man I've become right now
And I'm so glad that YOU were hired.

But why oh why are you standing here
And saying all of these things?
What made you come to life at all
And become a human being?

I heard some sounds coming from this room.
They penetrated my heart and my soul.
And then I started to breathe and move
And I found I had complete control.

I stepped quite carefully toward the music.
I wanted to hear more and more.
I saw you were sleeping quietly
When I peeked through a crack in the door.

I needed to get to those heavenly sounds.
As I neared the player, it knew
That I needed the music to get louder and louder
Even if it awakened you.

The tones and chords of that sonata, well
It's as if they were speaking to me.
It's as if I was here for this very moment
To be what I should be.

I know now that musical notes, all musical sounds
Will be everything to me.
It will be my desire and my devotion in life
And soon everyone will see.

Before you finally awakened
I stood here for quite some time.
I carefully studied the music I heard
And the notes and tones seemed to rhyme.

I have to be a part of this world.
I know this is where I belong.
I must learn to compose these things
And I must be a singer of songs.

The sculptor completely agreed with him
As his passion simply filled the room.
Now he knew he'd created a Masterpiece
And he was watching the Masterpiece bloom.

But he would never fulfill his dreams right here
In an old sculptor's studio.
He would have to leave to find his dream
And the old sculptor told him so.

So when you're ready and your heart tells you so
Just leave whenever you wish.
You'll know when the time is perfect and right
But first let me tell you this.

You'll live for all of the moments
You can sing a composer's songs.
You'll relish the adoration of family and fans
The world is where you belong.

Choose smartly and wisely along the way.
Choose friends that will have your back.
Your parents and family will give their support
And help with the things you may lack.

You'll be amazed at the love you'll receive
And not just for your heavenly singing.
But for the humble person you'll become
And because of the love you'll be bringing.

The Masterpiece thanked the sculptor
For the confidence he portrayed.
And asked if he could rest a while
Before his departure was made.

Of course, please rest right here on this bed.
I'll take my comfortable place.
Sleep well and have some pleasant dreams.
You'll have some decisions to face.

These kindred souls now rested a bit.
It had been an interesting day.
He'd created a singular Masterpiece
From some molds that had been on display.

The hours passed and the sun shone through
The windows to his right.
But the sculptor found as he opened his eyes
That the Masterpiece was nowhere in sight.

He quickly checked the studio
He even went outside.
He asked his wife if she'd seen someone
And she very smartly replied.

There's been no one here except you and me
I've been by your side all along.
The illness you have been battling with
Has put you to sleep for too long.

You never saw a nice looking man
That stood about six foot three?
You're saying I've been asleep all the while?
Please tell me you're kidding me!

Honey, I think you should go back to bed.
You're clearly not ready to wake.
If you think there's been a gentleman here
Then it's surely been your mistake.

But please go look at the studio.
You'll see where I used my tools.
You'll see the remnants of clay all around
And my glasses are on the stool.

But Dear I'm sorry to tell you this
But the studio looks just fine.
You haven't sculpted for a solid month
Unless I am going blind.

Well, perhaps it was a dream, I guess
But as vivid as it could be.
I know this Masterpiece exists somewhere
And how wondrous he will be.

I know you won't ever believe this
Since you think I've been seeing things.
But when that man appears to the world
It's because of the songs he will sing.

His voice will be astonishing.
The people will claim, "He's the best"!
And he'll be a bringer of love and peace
And will tower above the rest.

What a marvelous, marvelous dream to have
And if this man really does exist.
I'm telling you when you hear him sing
You'll feel like your soul's been kissed.

I still want to believe he was here for a day
And formed from clay I could feel.
I'm telling you honey. I'm telling you now.
That the Masterpiece is real.

Pamela McGee Wilkinson
January 4, 2021

Yes, Virginia, there is a Santa Claus
And yes world, the Masterpiece is real.

UNFORGETTABLE DAYS
By DIMASH KUDAIBERGEN

with some help from Pamela Wilkinson (and the influence of millions of Dears through the science of osmosis which rhymes with Dimashitosis which again is the reason for another poem. Somebody stop me! Please!)

My childhood home was a place for growth
And love was part of it all
And Singing and Music of every kind
Were common within those walls

There were gatherings and gatherings
of family and friends year after year after year
They filled our home with laughter and song
They are precious to me and dear

When the Lady of Music became my focus
I was barely a child of two
She consumed my every waking thought
And even while dreaming too

As the years went by
I practiced and studied to magnify my art
I put aside so many things
But still loved it with all of my heart

My neighborhood friends used to tease me
For singing in notes too high
They seemed to enjoy instructing me
To just sing like a tenor guy

But how do you stop what comes naturally
Or pretend that it doesn't exist
If God gives you talents to use and increase
You don't reject the gifts

So I continued to sing those singular notes
And way past maturation
and because of God's gifts and blessings to me
those notes became a sensation

I have parents, teachers and coaches to thank
And Allah of course was My Friend
He was there with me from the very beginning
and will be with me till the end.

This journey I am on is a whirlwind
A pairing of concerts and dears
My band and my singers and dancers
Calm my worries and opening night fears

My grandparents and parents have done so much
to prove that they'll always be there
It is my goal to make them proud
And show them how much I care.

My Dears are part of my family
who adorn me with love and support
They love to hear of my daily adventures
So I always post and report

I want them all to join me
And become an essential part
Of my magical musical mystery tour
And stay within my heart

We've proven together that the Lady of Music
Has no limits of borders or states
She gathers us all within her reach
And invites us to her estate

When I have some time to remember
These unforgettable days
I think of that boy in Aktobe
And wonder in so many ways

Did he ever, ever, ever imagine
that this would be his lot?
To sing for the sheer love of singing
I'm certain that he could not.

So I'll say to that boy from Aktobe
Just look at what you've made
Your dreams of singing for the world
Have shaped unforgettable days.

P.S. Dimash
If these are not your sentiments
Forgive me
I guess I was thinking of someone else.

Pam of Utah
December 9, 2020

BEFORE AND AFTER

"There are moments which mark your life. Moments when you realize nothing will ever be the same and time is divided into two parts, before this…and after this."

Dears,
I would love to take credit for this quote but I wrote it down after watching a movie over a decade ago and have used this many times to emphasize to myself and others that certain moments in our lives change us, sometimes dramatically, and we become different, sometimes for the better and sometimes…. not so much.

I believe I can count those kinds of events on one hand. The last event started the night I heard Dimash singing SOS for the first time. Obsession is only one way to describe all the characteristics of this event. I'm not sure THIS obsession of millions of fans is what Dimash intended but he needs to claim it nonetheless.

Perhaps Dimash's last moment like this was the day after SOS was revealed to a Chinese television audience in early 2017. He has said as much in several interviews. He's on a journey and he's taking us with him and we are bringing with us all the love, respect and admiration that he deserves but never ever expected or dreamed about.

Pam of Utah
4 DEC 2020

SUPERCALIFRAGILISTICWITHDIMASHITOSIS

PAM WONDERS....about

My Dimashitosis ....which was diagnosed on February 10, 2019, on that show whose name I will not speak, has reared its ugly head again and I am once again compelled to share its latest symptom with you dears. Because....if I like sitting in my recliner enjoying my retired lifestyle, I can't possibly share it with family or they will quietly put me away.

Current symptom .... LYRIC WRITING

When I heard this Disney song this morning, I asked myself...how can I turn that into a Dears' theme song for Dimash Kudaibergen? A legitimate question. I'm sure you've all asked it!

So here it is and if you're under 20 and you don't know how to sing this song because you haven't been introduced to Disney movies, then Google it or go ask your grandmother. Grandmothers know everything! I'm living proof.

SUPERCALIFRAGILISTIC
WITH DIMASHITOSOS

SupercalifragilisticwithDimashitosis
We will never conquer this
because he is the Mostest
SupercalifragilisticwithDimashitosis
SupercalifragilisticwithDimashitosis

This guy named Kudaibergen
had a dream that he would be
the greatest singer in the world
go down in history
with great determination
he would realize his fate
By singing vocal ranges
that included a D8. Oh!

SupercalifragilisticwithDimashitosis
We will never conquer this
because he is the Mostest
SupercalifragilisticwithDimashitosis
SupercalifragilisticwithDimashitosis

Um-diddle-diddle-diddle-um-diddleye
Um-diddle-diddle-diddle-um-diddleye

He traveled all around the world
and everywhere he'd go
There were a million dears around
to see his every show
The dears would come from every clime
from Maine to Timbuktu
To hear this Singer sing his songs
While gaping at the view. Oh!

SupercalifragilisticwithDimashitosis
We will never conquer this
because he is the Mostest.
SupercalifragilisticwithDimashitosis
SupercalifragilisticwithDimashitosis

Um-diddle-diddle-diddle-um-diddleye
Um-diddle-diddle-diddle-um-diddleye

Our Sinful Passion knows no bounds
But we will not complain
He doesn't Know the spell he casts
From Timbuktu to Maine
We hope he never figures out
the wonder of his ways
For every time we see this gent
He sets our hearts ablaze! Oh!

SupercalifragilisticwithDimashitosis
We will never conquer this
because he is the Mostest

SupercalifragilisticwithDimashitosis
SupercalifragilisticwithDimashitosis

Um-diddle-diddle-diddle-um-diddleye
Um-diddle-diddle-diddle-um-diddleye

What is this phenomenon
That haunts us night and day
Dears across the world
Are simply puzzled and dismayed
When we're not watching videos
he's singing in our brains
We think he plots and plans each move
To drive us all insane. Oh!

SupercalifragilisticwithDimashitosis
We will never conquer this
because he is the Mostest
SupercalifragilisticwithDimashitosis
SupercalifragilisticwithDimashitosis

(Big ending with an E6 or an E7 if you can pull it off.
Just kidding.)

SUPER CALI FRAGILISTIC
WITH DIMASHI TOSIS !
(keep singing the chorus until someone threatens intervention then you will Know you're a true Dear)

Credit to the composer of this Disney Classic
Pam of Utah
December 2, 2020

TO BE(ARD) OR NOT TO BE(ARD) THAT IS THE QUESTION.....

(A poem about facial growth and its consequences for Dimash)
(P.S. That is the only funny line. The rest of the time I am dead serious.)

WITH beard or no beard
For him it's just a choice
But with beard or no beard
The Dears sure have their voice.

WE LOVE you our Prince Dimash
No matter what's on your face
Be it hair, sweat, soot, or a leaf
Whatever is the case.

SHAVING is a choice men make
The occasion is the key
"Should I do this or that with this growth?
I'll guess I'll just wait and see."

SO be yourself, your awesome self
And share the things you will
We'll wait right here till kingdom come
For every film or still.

THE Dears cannot explain
The HOLD you have on us
But while we try to figure this out
Just let us make our fuss.

THIS fandom thing has us perplexed
But we're in good company
We've come from every walk of life
And from sea to shining sea.

YOUR winning smile, infectious laugh
Can bring us to our knees
We'll love you to the moon and back
So hear this mantra please.

YOUR music and your honesty
Is there in every frame
We see the person you've become
You may have God to blame.

JUST keep on posting pictures
And we'll melt, smile or we'll laugh
You are our beautiful Prince Dimash
In every photograph.

27 November 2020

PAM WONDERS ABOUT....

THINGS I DON'T UNDERSTAND

Number one: Why anyone would prefer thin Oreos over double stuffed. Boggles my mind.

Number two: How a plane, any plane, stays up in the air and gets from point A to point B.

Number three: What infinity really means.

Number four: Why absence makes the heart grow fonder. Seems like it would do the opposite.

Number five: Why someone says they will do something and never do.

Number six: Why anyone could hear Dimash Kudaibergen perform one song and not become some form of "obsessed" with his talent. That REALLY boggles my mind.

(These are only 10% of the things I don't understand.)

Have a nice day or evening.

25 NOVEMBER 2020

CURIOUS BY NATURE
23 November 2020

I am curious by nature. When I was young starting around 9 or 10, I used to hang around with the adults at the dinner table and listen to them talk, mesmerized by their knowledge and viewpoints and their take on life as they shared their opinions on many different matters.

I'm kind of an interviewer by nature also. Asking questions so that I can get into the heart of the matter that I might be discussing with a friend or acquaintance. Essentially, I need the details for my puzzle.

So naturally, being an avid fan, which is putting it mildly, of Dimash Kudaibergen, I have many questions that float around in my mind but I don't know where to find the answers unless I can ask the man himself which is probably never going to happen.

So I'm going to ask the dears if they know, not think they know, but if they know the answers to these questions. So here we go:

1. Is there any definitive information out there when Dimash performed for the first time, as a solo singer, with a complete orchestra? For example, the date or his age at the time, the occasion or venue and how many were in the audience? Because when that happened for him, it had to be a milestone that he reached that was so satisfying and appreciated and perhaps beyond his ability to comprehend. I can only imagine how the gratitude speech at the end of his song(s) to the maestro and orchestra went.
2. On a daily basis most of us dears watch his video performances and of course 98.7% of the time they are pure perfection. The other 1.3 % are just plain old everyday perfection. But I'm wondering if he ever has to do a second take or third take because he reached for one of those notes that he couldn't hit for some reason (and every singer has plenty of reasons) and therefore another take or recording was necessary. I'm only wondering because it almost defies all reason that even Dimash Kudaibergen could have a perfect performance in one take each and every time.

3. When and where is the most recent interview where he volunteers the info or is asked about how much and how often he practices his vocals. I have heard before that it's 3 to 4 hours daily but I'm wondering because of his crazy schedule if that's even possible anymore.
4. I'm also curious if there is available a 6'3" standing cardboard cut out of Dimash Kudaibergen and where a person could buy one. I'm asking for a friend. She lives alone and could use the company.
5. Does anyone know what Dimash naturally smells like? Or if there is a company that could replicate his smell into an essential oil for a diffuser? Again, asking for a friend.

That's all I have for now. Thanks
Pam of Utah

A DAY IN THE LIFE OF A DEAR

Part 3 of our mysterious disease.

(Which defies all semblance of credulity and may be the end stage of Dimashitosis. Intervention is the ONLY cure.)

SCENE: A DEAR'S LIVING ROOM

A friend stops by to visit a friend who just happens to be a Dear of three years.

Friend: How are you doing?

Dear: I'm better now that Dimash has a new song coming out... uh...soon.

Friend: Oh really. We're starting out with him again? Well, you said you were feeling better now. Were you not feeling so great?

Dear: Well, before I heard about the new song coming out, I was a wreck because I heard he had a cold.

Friend: So you were upset because your singer guy had a cold?

Dear: Yes!!!! It's a big deal when he has a cold. Poor baby.

Friend: So apparently you're better and he's better, I guess, and he's announced a new song. Can we move on to something else?

Dear: Well, yes, I guess we can try.

Friend: So my daughter won a regional drama contest this past weekend and…..

Dear: Oh, that's nothing. Dimash has won first place in every contest he has ever entered since he was six with only one exception. Poor Baby!

Friend: That's nice. So my daughter was up against 12 other contestants and……

Dear: Just 12? My Dimash has competed against 100 at one time and dozens and dozens during other contests and always came out on top…except for that one other time of course.

Friend: Can I please just finish telling you about my daughter's competition?

Dear: Again, I guess you can try.

Friend: It was a dramatic interpretation and she was playing three characters at once and had to use three different voices and when the judge…

Dear: Just three different voices? Really? My Dimash SINGS with 15 different voices in ONE song! He can sing off of the piano from the left end all the way to the right end. Do you even KNOW what a D8 is?

Friend: You know what, never mind. Do you have something to eat like an apple or a banana? I haven't had lunch yet and I'm starving.

Dear: I have plenty of pears but I'm out of snacky things.

Friend: Just pears? Not my favorite fruit. Okay….so do you have anything to drink?

Dear: I have room temperature colas.

Friend: Room temperature? Can I have a glass with some ice in it?

Dear: Cold cola? Okay, but that sounds like a stupid combination.

Friend: You know what, never mind. Uh...how is your husband?

Dear: Who??

Friend: Randall! Randall! Your husband!

Dear: Oh, him. I guess he's okay. I think his diverticulitis is in check or he may need surgery. I forget. But now that Dimash is over his cold and his new song is coming out....

Friend: Wait! Wait! Why do you always return to that singer fellow when we were clearly talking about something else?

Dear: I don't do that. Do I do that? When do I do that?

Friend: (Clearly exasperated) The whole time I have been here! That's when!

Dear: Speaking of "time" and "when".....what do you think the definition of "soon" is? Like how much time IS soon? Is it a few hours? A few weeks? Surely it's not a few months!?!?! Tell me it's not a few months!

Friend: (Looking at her cell phone for the time) You know what? I forgot I have a colonoscopy in a few minutes. I better get going.

Dear: A colonoscopy? You're not supposed to eat OR drink before a colonoscopy. Why did you ask for a pear and a warm cola?

Friend: I didn't ask for...oh never mind. Running late. See ya.

Dear: Oh, okay. The next time we visit and you have a bit more time, I'll tell you all about Dimash and the time he was eating a pear in an airport in China. It's the best story ever! It's a great idea for a movie.

I think Dimash should play himself. Don't you? Good luck with your pedicure.

Friend: Sure. Sure. (Mumbles to herself..."Oh for the sweet relief of a colonoscopy.")

The End
Pam of Utah 20 November 2020

DIMASHITOSIS DIAGNOSIS

PART TWO....Dears...it gets worse

PAM'S WONDERING.....about DIMASHITOSIS ???

Do you have THESE side effects? If so, it's not looking good....

Check WebMD pages 152 - 154

Apparently, some dears have SEVERE cases of Dimashitis that only WebMD could define and diagnose. For help call 1-KAZ-524-1994 (get it?) and ask for Dimash since it's all his dad gum fault.

DIMASHITOSIS is the chronic incurable condition of a fan, typically female, of Dimash Kudaibergen (the famed young singer from Kazakhstan; see Wikipedia) who has taken the obsession of his music, his looks, his performance genius, his looks, his humble personality, his looks, and a few other things like his LOOKS to such a level that she actually considers kidnapping. See # 11 Below.

1. You know you're in trouble when you start giving each of your goose bumps a name ......and run out of names.
2. Trying to sing phonetically his Kazakh song "Unforgettable Day" day after day after day after day after unforgettable day...... until you just give up and go watch him sing it. It's probably wise.
3. Trying to find a place in your heart to believe him when he says "I am just an ordinary guy" but dismissing that statement because sometimes he just really doesn't know what he's talking about.

4. You're still giving Dimash the benefit of the doubt that he may have "accidentally" forgot to wear a T-shirt to bed before he took that bedroom selfie and posted it on his IG.
5. Thanking all the Greek Gods that ever lived and ever will live that Dimash may have "accidentally" forgot to wear a T-shirt to bed before he took that bedroom selfie and posted it on his IG.
6. Spending too much of your free time mentally thanking Dimash for "intentionally" forgetting to wear a T-shirt to bed before he took that selfie and posted it on his IG.
7. Wondering how much money you could make on Amazon by selling "invisible socks" (his second favorite kind of socks to wear) with an invisible DK embroidered on them.

Pros and Cons of Invisible DK socks from Amazon include

Pro: Free overnight shipping and handling to Madagascar. (It's an Amazon thing. Take it up with Jeff Bezos.)

Pro: They never need washing because you can never find them.

Con: You can never find them.

Con: They cost $65.00 a pair because of the invisible embroidery.

Another Pro: Shipping and handling charges are never added to your credit card because what company in their right mind would ever send you an invisible ...ANYTHING? (What you don't see is what you don't get.)

8. Cursing Dimash under your breath (PG only) each time he sends an eye-candy photo and says "Good Night". What in the world is going to be GOOD about it? Can someone please tell me?
9. Curious if your severe case of Dimashitosis could get you out of Jury Duty.
10. Back to the sexy bedroom selfie: Wondering if it truly was a selfie or did he get Mansur to take the picture...and if so ...was Dimash contributing to the delinquency of a minor? I'm just sayin'......
11. Convincing yourself after weeks and weeks of considering it

that kidnapping Dimash Kudaibergen is OK as long as you eventually return him where you stole him, I mean "found him" without a hair on his head disturbed. (Wait....What? If you didn't do at least that much, what were you thinking? Geez! Rookie!!!)
12. Seriously considering putting your puppy up for adoption because although he's chewed everything from your favorite household slippers to your $650 Louboutin designer pumps...destroying beyond recognition the DQ cap you bought in New York was definitely the last straw. Also, you can't find your NY lanyard and the perpetrator is a given. Seriously, get rid of the puppy.
13. Lamenting the fact that "SOON" doesn't always mean as 'soon' as you think it does.
14. And lastly, to be more precise and succinct and at some considerable risk of repeating yourself, not feeling guilty AT ALL for EVERY "really nice" thought you have ever HAD, are HAVING and will HAVE about that man.

Again, see the Helpline above if you need someone to blame since WebMD did not offer a cure. They did infer that it could be years and years.

****The fans have also inferred that the cure for too much Dimash is obviously MORE Dimash.

November 17, 2020

DIMASHITIS

PAM'S WONDERING.....

Do you have DIMASHITIS ? Check the....Worldwide Dictionary of Celebrity-Itis and find out:

See Page 26 Columns 4, 5, 6 and 2/3rds of column 7

DIMASHITIS : A condition that will generally develop after a human being is exposed to the musical talents and charismatic personality of one, Dimash Kudaibergen, a 26 year old man of Kazakhstan who is considered to be the greatest singer of all time.

Common, but not all inclusive, side effects are:

Watching his videos over and over and over and over again and actually caring what other people think about his videos by watching reactors and vocal coaches over and over and over and over again. And..... wondering if bragging about watching Sinful Passion 892 times is something to brag about or a good reason for an intervention from your family.

Failure to read the lyrics of the song as he is singing because you don't give a hoot at the time because you must concentrate on Every breath he takes. Every move he makes. Every step he takes. Every sound he makes. Every earth that shakes. Because you will be watching him (kind of really really closely).

Shortness of breath or just forgetting to breathe while you are watching him and trying to read the lyrics. Seriously, you cannot do both at the same time.

Keeping a fan nearby or an ice pack for a quick cool down.

Checking your pulse regularly to see if you are still alive.

Checking your purse regularly to see if you have any funds set aside for more Dimash merch.

Keeping tissues available at all times before you begin to watch him as it is inevitable that they will be necessary.

Ignoring all aspects of your life, i.e. food, water, sleep, bathroom breaks, work, children, husbands, all your relatives and friends, Doctors' appointments, World events such as pandemics, stock market dips, recessions and wars so you can watch said videos over and over again.

Practically making him your new religion (now that's bad, by the way!) He would not like that. This is when he would say "Get a grip!"

Forgetting your name, your age, your gender, the color of your hair, your mother's maiden name, what kind of car you drive, your best friend's name or that you even had a best friend.

Communicating for days and weeks and months at a time with only dears from your several fan clubs.

Forgetting what life was like before Dimashitis set in. Here's where that BEFORE DIMASH AND AFTER DIMASH phenomenon is born.

Forgetting to take your medication for Dimashitis ....which if it actually existed, you would forget to take it anyway because what Dear in her (okay, his too) right mind would want a cure.

Bringing up Dimash Kudaibergen to your doctor, your dentist, your veterinarian, your lawyer, your pastor or Bishop, the clerk at the grocery store, your Uber driver, the Dominoe's pizza boy, because you just can't stand it if they don't know WHO Dimash Kudaibergen Is!!

Handing a print out of go-to songs of his to the above. (Print outs are in this book)

Making bargains with your friends, if you still have any, that you will clean their house for a month if they would just listen to three of his songs in your presence.

Promising someone you will only talk about Dimash for five minutes and 55 minutes later you're still talking.

Finding it difficult to go back in your memory banks to remember the singers you used to listen to before Dimashitis set in.

Wondering if this disease will ever play out in your mind, your heart and your soul and hoping that it never will. This is called a conundrum or a dichotomy.

Wondering why you haven't packed your bags and moved to Kazakhstan for heaven's sake and if stalking him is a good or bad idea (or against the law) in Nur-Sultan.

Removing your country's flag on patriotic holidays and replacing it with the flag of Kazakhstan.

A pear, almost overnight, becomes your favorite fruit.

You are looking for Dimash Kudaibergen in ANY airport because..... you never know and ...bringing a bouquet of flowers...just in case.

Keeping an album of Dimash pictures in your camera file on your phone and wondering if 1,272 pictures are a bit much.

Telling your friends, again, if you still have any, that if they can't tell you what YOUR five favorite Dimash songs are, then they are dead to you.

Purchasing every Dimash Kudaibergen perfume, t-shirt, hat, magnetic whatevers, a license plate, teas, a dombra that you will never learn to play, lanyards, stickers, all the D and K and Q letters that Hobby Lobby sells, plane tickets, concert tickets, sharing a hotel room with a perfect stranger.

Spending hours typing REQUEST DIMASH.

Not feeling guilty for every thought you have ever had about the man.

THE END...FOR NOW!

Pam of Utah

(P.S. Do not bother googling the Worldwide Dictionary of Celebrity-Itis. It does not exist.)

14 November 2020

Okay...here I go again...

If you're following Dimash's various interviews over time, you've heard him say to us something to the effect....

"Don't focus so much on the octaves I can deliver but how I affect your emotions and take you to another world".

Yes, we appreciate your desire here, Dimash, but asking us to focus only on the *feelings* is like telling a guy to stare at a picture of Marilyn Monroe for five minutes and only look at her face! Geez!

Pam of Utah
14 November 2019

THE ARNAU BREAKDOWN

I keep telling myself… "Self, take a break from posting for just a few days" and then I break my promise because something happens and since I only have a sister I can share things with occasionally and certainly not every day, I automatically think of all of You who are in the same boat that I am in.

Literally a few minutes ago it's mid-morning Utah time and I've caught up with current events, and every American knows what that means, and I'm going to take a break from the Korean dramas that I love and just listen to Dimash.

Maybe I'll start with part 1 of the New York concert ….and as soon as that thought traveled from my brain and out of my mouth, I started crying and then crying turned into bawling. Memories of NY came flooding back. This has happened more times than I can count. I'll just think about one of his songs and before I can look it up…I'm crying… because I'm not sure I can handle those sweet, perfect emotions that pour out of me when I watch that man sing and perform.

I remember a Dimash video with him and some of the dears on a tram at an airport and lucky for them, he sang a few lines from one of his songs. And one of the dears said "Oh Dimash that was wonderful !" He replied "Oh no it wasn't". And I believe he meant it because he is that modest.

What???

Here's the thing! I'm not sure that he really realizes the effect his whole persona as well as his Heavenly voice has on us Dears.

I know he has said numerous times "Octaves, I don't care about the octaves. I just want to take you to a different place when you hear me sing."

Well that's just fine Dimash Kudaibergen but WHERE are you taking us?

All of us had/have never been there before and it seems so strange and foreign yet beautiful and exotic all at the same time.

It would almost be like looking at the most beautiful vista on the planet (and let's just assume it's somewhere in Kazakhstan) while you're eating the best piece of chocolate cake you've ever had and an eagle flies over your head and screeches "hello and have a nice day" and whoever was/is your favorite movie star is standing next to you holding your cold glass of milk.

Dang it ...THAT won't even come close.

So I shared ...and I may have garnered enough courage to watch Part 1. We will see.

I just HOPE that while he has been lamenting over the fact that he can't be on stage perhaps anytime soon, that he can find comfort and satisfaction in the fact that he has accomplished so much in the last decade of his life creating, performing and recording and producing millions of flustered dears who can't explain if their lives depended on it what he has done to them.

I hope. We all HOPE!
Pam of Utah
29 OCTOBER 2020

JUST A GUY FROM KAZAKHSTAN/THE PEAR POEM
(A poem about a pear. Yes, a pear!) October 24, 2020
By Dimash Kudaibergen {not really, of course}

The Weibo account from a lovely dear
Had views going through the roof.

They said it broke a record in views
But I'd have to see the proof.

A green juicy everyday fruit
A fruit you eat and forget.
It was JUST a pear, a pear, my dears
And certainly not worth all the fret.

An airport walk with fruit in hand
Gathered millions and millions of views?
I'm still scratching my Kazakh head at this
And am wondering what to do.

Should I invest in pears and other fruits
And send their shares to a climb?
Or just leave that plan to someone else
Cause I've really not got the time.

I love those walks, those airport walks.
Those dears really make my day.
But I'll watch what I eat or drink I guess
Cause they'll always have something to say.

Like one dear said and not in jest
"Don't eat THE CORE, my gosh!
The DNA on that remaining pear
Could make another Dimash!"

I'm puzzled that they watch me so close
And listen to all I speak.
They focus on every facial tic
And discuss them ALL for a week.

This event unfolded before my eyes
The media just blew it apart.
But in the end it proved to me
The Dears really have my whole heart.

I've said this before and I'll say it again
I'm blessed to have every fan
I consider myself the luckiest guy

JUST A GUY FROM KAZAKHSTAN.

PERSON(ALIZED) LICENSE PLATE

I have never ever considered buying a personalized plate and I have never considered advertising anything on my car with a magnetic "whatever" until… You know who(m)!

This 13-year-old Avalon has never looked more beautiful to me.

I should remember and believe I will always remember that I installed these plates (we get two of them for front and back in Utah) the day before his debut on MTV.

DIMASH1……?

If someone asks me what the 1 is for, I will just state the obvious. He's the Number 1 singer on the planet. Let me tell you about him. Six hours later, they will beg me to shut up.

Maybe I will. Maybe I won't.

Pam of Utah
1 October 2020

I AM MUSIC MY LICENSE PLATE

MY LEAF POEM
By DImash "Soon" Kudaibergen

(Not really.....but we can pretend it is)

I took this picture with a leaf
The cameraman said..."Here!"
I said "Okkkaaayyy. Let's do this thing."
But now it's tickling my ear.

The leaf's okay I guess
The color looks great with black
But why a leaf? I ask myself
Erlan will give me some flack.

The things I must do to please my Dears,
My agents, my staff, my crew!
I'd be here all day to count the ways
Because they are not.....just a few.

Modeling days, interviews
Traveling from here to Beijing
When all I want, what I really really want
Is to SING....is to SING....is to SING!

You'll never understand my motives
No one will ever get in my mind
The thoughts I am always thinking
Are always the singing kind.

I'm always singing in the shower
(Oops, be careful....my darling Dears)
And in cars, in hallways, even downtown
Wherever there's human ears.

But posing and posing with props and such
Is a price that I must spend
It comes with the job and so I must
I'll take the leaf and just pretend....

That I'm hugging my mic, my favorite mic

I've even named it Mick
It goes with me everywhere and anywhere
In case I need it quick.

I'm also thinking I'm hugging a Dear
Who traveled from afar
To listen to me sing on stage
And make me feel like a star.

So I thank that cameraman for giving me the leaf
That silky leaf of green
I am blessed! I am truly, truly blessed
With people and places and things.

So if I ever, ever look out of whack
While posing with..... ANYTHING!!!!
Please know, please always know...I'll be okay
AS SOON AS I CAN SING !!!

Pam of Utah
September 23, 2020
With love to DKK

A LEAGUE OF HIS OWN

Dimash Kudaibergen
A Gift from God
A paragon, a peacemaker, a mystery.

Dimash Kudaibergen
A Man of Kazakhstan
A patriot, a companion, a friend.

Dimash Kudaibergen
A Man from Aktobe
A grandson, a son and a brother.

Dimash Kudaibergen
A Man of Song
A musician, a composer, a director.

Dimash Kudaibergen
An Incarnation of gratitude
A nobler, a saint, and blessed.

Dimash Kudaibergen
A League of his Own
Our angel, our gift, our treasure.
A Thank You to Dimash

By Pamela Wilkinson/Pam of Utah
August 10, 2020

To Dimash

THE FATHER OF SONGS

What do you feed a brain that only runs on Music?
How do you keep it going?
What should you drink or eat to keep the music flowing?

What happens to the blood
When veins are filled with Lyrics?
How do you keep it there?
What happens to the heart
that's filled with Passion and waiting to be shared
Who knows the path a singer must tread
to share A Heavenly Tune?
Is it time and effort and sweat and tears
From morn till afternoon?

Do creative juices and inspiration
play a special part? Where do they fall in line?
Are they the engineers of our Singer's gift
to make our world sublime?

The Father of Songs knows these things
and knows them very well.
But keeps this knowledge to himself
and will never never tell.

We honor him his silence
of the secrets of his art
And thank him for his longing
to reach the human heart.

Love you Dimash
Keep singing to our hearts
We're listening.
Pam of Utah
23 May 2020

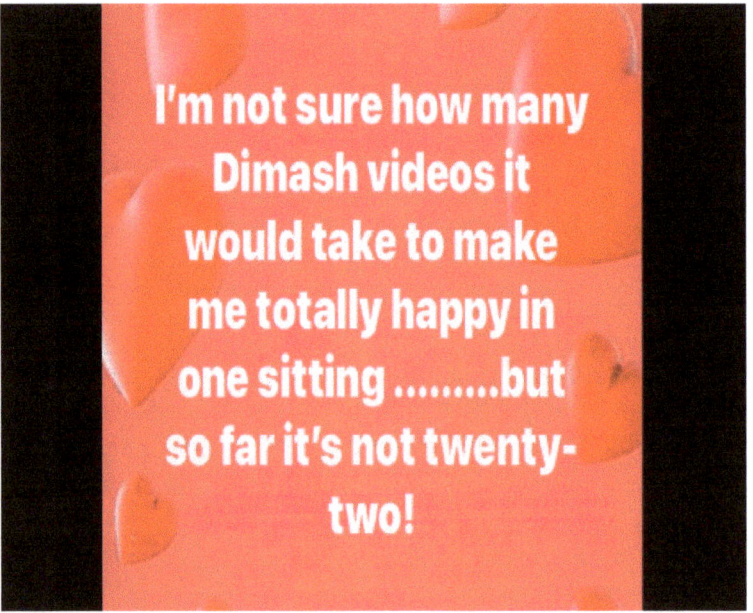

THE GOLDEN THROAT

This Kazakh man was born to sing
Like eagles were born to soar on wings
Blessed by God with a Golden Throat
He sings each song with golden notes.

He draws us in from far and near
Embraces us with words like "Dears"

Calms our souls and captures our hearts
This Golden Throat has done its part.

His tune, its tone, its power, his fame
Destiny had a hand in all he's gained
In time when all things are said and wrote
We'll revere the man with the Golden Throat.   20 May 2020

VERY PERSONAL JOURNAL ENTRY

Dears

I am a person that has always counted her blessings in life, past and present. Like most of you, if not all of you, life has brought me trials and heartaches, joy and satisfaction. Some of you know me by my sign-off on my posts as Pam of Utah. I used that sign-off because I was "borrowing" my husband's Facebook page because I never bothered to open one of my own. His friends and relatives and contacts are pretty much the same as mine so I used his for the last three years because he was diagnosed with Alzheimer's in 2017.

Using his Facebook page or even using his iPhone was very difficult those three years until he just gave up on them. On May 2 he died in a hospital in Salt Lake City due to complications of Alzheimer's and a couple of days later, I changed his Facebook page to mine, Pamela Wilkinson.

I appreciate you Dears but I do not want to make this about my loss. I know where he is and that we will be together again. But I do want to share with you as others have that this Amazing Singer that we love and admire so much has filled my long hours of downtime when my husband was sleeping or watching television with exquisite vocal renditions of amazing songs....without fail. Dang it, I'm crying as I'm dictating this.

My reluctant dear, Kenny, was with me in December as an audience member in the most amazing concert I have ever attended. I was so blessed during those four nights and five days to have him with me and to experience no real inconvenience with his presence and my responsibility to look after him. I ate breakfasts at the Holiday

Inn with several dears and got to know them a bit and they were so precious with my Kenny.

Now all of my life will be filled with whatever makes me happy and content and Dimash and his music will be at the top of that list. I'll have my church, my friends and family members from South Carolina to Oregon to fill those days too but some kid from Kazakhstan will be getting the lion's share of my time. It's your fault, Dimash! But thank you!

Signed, Pam of Utah 13 May 2020

PAM WONDERS.......WHATCHA THINKING DIMASH??

Well he's wondering if any of his dears can find all 20 hits listed below. It frees him from all of the other things he's thinking. Soooo......I was sitting in a restaurant enjoying chicken fingers and Texas toast for the first time in a long time, and not that chicken fingers aren't inspiring enough, but something made me think of a word search that contained Dimash Kudaibergen hits. Less than two minutes on the Internet and I'm making a word search happen. So just to give you something to do this weekend when you need to take a break from whatever, here you go. I'm hoping that you can figure out how to print this off. I made a screenshot of it and sent it to the printer. Enlarge it too for the visually impaired.

P.S. Make this challenging if you want. Time yourself and see how long it takes to find them all. Report your time if you wish to compete with other dears. I've already seen the answer key so I can't play. DANG!

PAM OF UTAH 5 December 2020

WORD SEARCH

A Dimash-20-Count Word Search

```
S F J U U E R P O I N P N S B Q K W K C Q Z D N U K O W X X
I U G V P A Z M U M M C B W V E F S Z W S P Z X O S M U Z G
V N E S F S M V R I O J V M E Z B T F G I M V H Q T Y Z D Y
Y X P W I Y M D L V X X F X Y A U C I R R N B T I Z S M D Y
M K H N I N P S O A K Q H U K B R B F A X G A M R S W R H L
U N G P M T F R V L Z G E J Z E E E P A M M S W H A A U F T
R S H F I K M U E Z Z D V L A S O A O W R O G I H V N H T R
Y F P M S A N D L T Y A B C E S E R U N N J C B I D H X C L
I J R D S H N O A P V T P C F D M A J T E E R O K D S Q W Y
F M D R Y P K B W Y A B W F C K W I Z D Y M N W S R X E M Y
C J A F O R Z J A C B S C K Y C F E N J D X C L T I W Q R M
N U W K U D Y C S U K R S S G K H P R E Q S G L J S I R E U
M S M V V P W D Y S W S E I I C A O W O K G G T K W M G A J
S T V L T F R X Z M Y P U A O J J X T O M G B C Q U A G L C
X L R U J K G A S E A A B Q K N K R Y H I A H C G A O K L O
K E E H R Z K L C P Z S Z A X N Z G L O O P E R A T W O B I
J T J T X V U P R Z M S Z G L C I W B O X L J T L J I P Y S
X I P D A J H N E I S I A P O H Q T S G G J X N R R X T M A
S T W N F N U F A U W O U Q W G Z M L H S N S T W L I Y Y O
R B R T L F M D M Q W N O W L D C O T Q Z F I M S M W J S P
R E V L X W Z N I H Z E V Y O U R L O V E O K P B P J S E Q
I J G J K V U B N B O B D T C C R W B H U X B V I J Y K L T
P V U F W H Y K G L L F M U N H H R W N Q W P G Q E L K F A
A C X Z H E S D Z R U X O W H G R H O S S W Z N U X T T L I
G Y T Q F O R R S L X Q F E K A F W U H P W L G J K Y R D D
G Z F T K P W W D G B Z R A W P R N E A G F V N Q G X D A K
O T U R W N L K F T N D Z Q C N J A L E D H A E G G R V V K
J S A S T Y F Z C H T H E C R O W N I K H V I N F R L R M Y
S O O X Z C F H F F C T C A S J Z A A U T U M N S T R O N G
J S V U I V O F F M I B M E W W S T W I R P N U P G G Y M E
```

SINFULPASSION	AUTUMNSTRONG	JUSTLETITBE	ALLBYMYSELF
OGNIPIETRA	SCREAMING	TIAMOCOSI	PASSIONE
MYBEAUTY	WEAREONE	THECROWN	IMISSYOU
DAYBREAK	YOURLOVE	OPERATWO	JASMINE
KNOW	OURLOVE	MYSWAN	SOS

DIMASH FLYER

Printed this off in fall 2019 to give out to Dimash-impaired individuals.

I tell them.... "This should get you started. Have fun!"

You can invent your own and even get a little creative with it. I've carried these with me since fall of 2019. Depending on the person, I've written my phone # on the back in case they want to know more from an "expert on Dimash".

ALL ABOUT <u>DIMASH KUDAIBERGEN</u>
IN 50 WORDS OR LESS; FIRST
CK HIM OUT ON WIKIPEDIA
THEN GO TO YOUTUBE AND TYPE IN
DIMASH S.O.S. SINGER 2017 FROM HIS
YOUTUBE CHANNEL; THEN OPERA 2
BEST VOICE IN THE WORLD; FANCAM
OGNI PIETRA; SINFUL PASSION NEW
WAVE 2018; LOVE IS LIKE A DREAM,
DIMASH KUDAIBERGEN

ALL ABOUT <u>DIMASH KUDAIBERGEN</u>
IN 50 WORDS OR LESS; FIRST
CK HIM OUT ON WIKIPEDIA
THEN GO TO YOUTUBE AND TYPE IN
DIMASH S.O.S. SINGER 2017 FROM HIS
YOUTUBE CHANNEL; THEN OPERA 2
BEST VOICE IN THE WORLD; FANCAM
OGNI PIETRA; SINFUL PASSION NEW
WAVE 2018; LOVE IS LIKE A DREAM,
DIMASH KUDAIBERGEN

ALL ABOUT <u>DIMASH KUDAIBERGEN</u>
IN 50 WORDS OR LESS; FIRST
CK HIM OUT ON WIKIPEDIA
THEN GO TO YOUTUBE AND TYPE IN
DIMASH S.O.S. SINGER 2017 FROM HIS
YOUTUBE CHANNEL; THEN OPERA 2
BEST VOICE IN THE WORLD; FANCAM
OGNI PIETRA; SINFUL PASSION NEW

WAVE 2018; LOVE IS LIKE A DREAM,
DIMASH KUDAIBERGEN

PAM'S FAVORITES IN ALPHABETICAL ORDER IN ORDER TO AVOID FAVORITISM OF ANY KIND

ACROSS ENDLESS DIMENSIONS
ADAGIO
ALL BY MYSELF
AUTUMN STRONG
CONFESSA
DAIDIDAU
DAYBREAK
DIVA DANCE
DRUNKEN CONCUBINE/DIVA DANCE
GIVE ME LOVE
GIVE ME YOUR LOVE
GOLDEN
HELLO
I COULDN'T LEAVE
I MISS YOU
IF I NEVER BREATHE AGAIN
JUST LET IT BE
KNOW
LAY DOWN
LEILA
LOVE IS LIKE A DREAM
LOVE OF TIRED SWANS
MADEMOISELLE HYDE
MARIGOLDS
MISS YOU
MOONLIGHT MAMA
MY BEAUTY
MY SWAN
OCEANS OVER TIME
OGNI PIETRA/OLIMPICO
ONLY YOU
OPERA 2
OUR LOVE

PASSIONE
QAIRAN ELIM
QARAGYM-AI
QUEEN MEDLEY
RESTART MY LOVE
S.O.S. D'UN TERRIEN EN DETRESSE
SAMALTAU
SCREAMING
SINFUL PASSION
THE CROWN
THE SHOW MUST GO ON
THOUSANDS OF MILES/A COMMON DREAM
TI AMO COSI
TU VAS ME DETRUIRE
UNFORGETTABLE DAY
WAR AND PEACE
YOUR LOVE
P.S. PAM.....IF YOU MISSED ANY, IT'S 4:15 A.M. AND WAY PAST YOUR BEDTIME

DEARS' COMMENTS

Some Comments from Dears that boosted my resolve to show my appreciation to Dimash by self-publishing my journey with him. I hope this doesn't seem self-serving but I wanted the readers to know that there was/is a genuine interest in me and others to publish their creative talents that show their appreciation to Dimash. So here are a few comments. Thanks again for your support.
Pamela

Re: There's something wrong with him
Sheesh, I sat down on the toilet (TMI) dutifully opened the fan club page (cuz what else am I supposed to do here?) and could not continue because I was laughing too hard at this post! Pam, you're killing me! Literally! Can't do normal bodily functions now, thanks to you!!

Mariana H.
(Sorry MH but this was too cute to pass up)...Pam

Re: Digital Dimash Magic

I just LOVE the way you think!! I'm also grateful that you SHARE it!

I say we need you to compile your poems for us! Will you do that, pretty please, and maybe PUBLISH them for us???

Shelley D.

Re: The Master's Repair

Pam, dear. I believe that you should have these poems printed in a hardcover book for public view and posterity. I'm sure Dimash would love to have a copy, as well as fellow dears, like me. Happy New Year. Keep them coming!

Madeline T

Thank you for this beautiful poem! I agree that you should publish these works!

Shirley G

Re: THE GIFT THAT KEEPS ON GIVING

That is again, an amazing poem. You managed to capture in words the inexplicable. Thanks for that! Time for a Dears and Dimash poetry book. It would sell out in an instant!!

Heidi

Oh sweet Dear Pamela. I have no words to describe how beautiful I found this poem. You seem to always 'knock the wind out of me' with the beauty of the very scenic presentation of the sentences. ((Well I see that you state that there are some of our comments in there)) but still, the way you put them together to wholeheartedly describe our beloved Kazakh prince of song and music, is so profound that it made me sit here with silent tears streaming down my face while reading every word, and my lips curved upwards to a proud smile. It is so well put together.. It's perfect.

Dania G.

Wow, another great example of your gift for poetry Pamela! I hope someday you will have a collection of your poems published and present one to Dimash. And also so I can buy one from you!
Debbie H.

(Thank you for the compliments. I hope to. Wink wink Pam)
Wonderful! Thank you for the gift of writing, Ms. Pam. Thank you, Dimash for the inspiration!
Mel

What a beautiful poem. I hope Dimash receives it. Every word is so true. I think we Dears all feel the same. Thank you Pamela for posting.
Jolie

But "You are much more to us than the sounds that come out of you "... Beautiful and says all there is to say about Dimash and Dears. Thank you, Pam of Utah.
Helga

So wonderful with words!! Thank you for sharing your talent. My mother was a poet too and your style reminds me of her ♥
Krissy

Re: I AM MUSIC
I noticed mine in there. Thanks Pam. He was born to sing - he WAS music, he IS music and he WILL FOREVER BE music. That is all I know and all I need to know.
Sheila

I am crying now, that is extraordinary.
Moldy Oldy

Reading your poems always make me cry like a child. They explain my experiences with him; they explain the high level of never known devotion. And for a while I am feeling normal with my willingness to catch a bullet for someone I never met. You always find such wonderful words to describe the emotions of us all. You're a true artist.

I'm literally waiting for your poems. ♥

Sabine

Sabine
Thank you so much Sabine
When inspiration hits and I'm writing these stanzas and I'm crying through some of them as they come out of my mouth and on my notebook app, I always have the feeling that someone else might pick up the spirit in those lines or the meaning behind them. Other than my church members that I have a lot in common with, I have never experienced this kind of connection with a large group of people where we understand each other fully. In reference to your looking forward to more poems, every time I write one I say to myself "OK that's it. I can't imagine anything else that could inspire me to write 14 to 31 stanzas. (My record now is 57 but such a joy to write) I feel like I've covered Dimash so thoroughly and then all of a sudden something happens …and here comes another one.
Pam

RE: THE SCULPTOR PT 1 (If my poems were my children, this is the child that I whisper to "You are my favorite but don't tell the others. Shhh.")
Pamela Wilkinson!

I hardly ever cry at a poem, but you … you made me do just that!

My breath was taken away … first it was cut short, I had to pick myself up and gasp for air, I could not believe my eyes.

The way the short sentences flowed through my mind made me realize … to start again, this time with my focus a full 100% alert.

Then I started again and I tell you … the quality MATCHES Dimash's being!

It is uncanny - I read it twice and again, goosebumps all over!

I'm actually going to read it out, aloud, in my phone, so I can play it, whenever I want!

My <3 heartfelt <3 greetings and so much thanks! ;).

Pukkie

RE: UNFORGETTABLE DAYS

Pam of Utah, you are quite a remarkable talent. Love your poems. Is there a book of poetry in the works?
Antonia

Pamela Wilkinson I bet if your book of poetry was all about Dimash & included his pictures & philosophical quotes it would sell like hotcakes!
Antonia

RE: SUPERCALIFRAGILISTICWITHDIMASHITOSIS

Thank you Pam.. This is so good I can't stop singing it...btw intervention for my lost soul has been scheduled by my friend (she got worried about my sanity when she noticed that I kept singing and forgot about drinking my coffee...again) Chely
Chely

This goes without saying, I'm sure, but it looks like you may have traded one addiction for another. Pam
Pamela Wilkinson I love how your mind works. More than that, I'm SO glad you share it!!
Erma Bombeckish
Shelley D.

www.ingramcontent.com/pod-product-compliance
Lightning Source LLC
LaVergne TN
LVHW051225070526
838200LV00057B/4611